T0065245

PATHWAYS TO ACHIEVING YOUR FULLEST POTENTIAL

Develop the power that resides in you and make yourself grow into your best edition ever!

DR. ARTEMIO B. CABAHUG

PATHWAYS TO ACHIEVING YOUR FULLEST POTENTIAL DEVELOP THE POWER THAT RESIDES IN YOU AND MAKE YOURSELF GROW INTO YOUR BEST EDITION EVER!

iUniverse books may be ordered through booksellers or by contacting:

iUniverse
1663 Liberty Drive
Bloomington, IN 47403
www.iuniverse.com
844-349-9409

ISBN: 978-1-5320-9208-4 (sc)
ISBN: 978-1-5320-9209-1 (e)

Library of Congress Control Number: 2020921984

Print information available on the last page.

iUniverse rev. date: 11/30/2020

CONTENTS

ABOUT THE AUTHOR

 Dr. Artemio Cabahug, DM, has over 35 years of extensive experience in the practice and teaching of office administration and human resource management in the Philippines and in the Middle East. As a fresh B.S. commerce graduate of the University of San Jose Recoletos in Cebu City in 1981, the young Archietim taught marketing and management at the PAFCA College in Lapu-Lapu City for one year. He then put up a handicraft business producing coconut-shell and seashell fashion accessories for export, but he closed it down after starting to work in the Middle East for a two-year overseas contract as field worker, operating a huge jackhammer for an electrification project in the Wadi Dawasir desert in Riyadh. He was moved by his employer to its survey team and later to its main office as computer assistant for the remaining six months of his contract. Then he worked on a two-year contract as executive secretary with a Jeddah-based construction firm owned by a Saudi Arabia's Prince

That contract over in 1990, Archietim flew back to his homeland and studied at the University of the Philippines for his Master's in business management as a university scholar, doing so while he worked as marketing manager and systems consultant for a Cebu City computer-telecom services firm. In 1993, the lure of overseas contract work took him back to the Middle East when he was recruited as executive secretary and administrative project head for an Al-Khobar-based consulting firm that assigned him to service Saudi Aramco, the world's biggest oil producer. The firm subsequently assigned him to Saudi Aramco itself in Jeddah as executive secretary in a contractual engagement that lasted seven years until 2000. Archietim then flew back to the Philippines but in 2001, he accepted a contract offer by another consultancy firm servicing Saudi Aramco, this time as senior project support supervisor based in Al-Khobar. He worked for the firm for more than three years but no longer renewed his contract, deciding to go back to the Philippines for good. In 2008, he obtained his doctorate in human resources management from the University of San Jose Recoletos.

*This book is dedicated to my beautiful and
talented daughter, Ranya Dhelle
and to my brilliant, hardworking and very obedient son, Keene Krasi.*

*Also, I dedicate this book to my favorite client, Mr. Alfrito
D. Mah, President and CEO of six big corporations
in the Philippines, for a relationship that
has gone beyond business to a very close friendship
that endures until today.*

FOREWORD

Over a decade ago, I discovered the business wisdom of Dr. Artemio Cabahug. It was through his educational and inspiring column in *Sunstar Pampanga*, a daily broadsheet where he was a guest columnist on human resource development. His "Managing People in the Workplace" columns demonstrated his deep understanding of human behavior in organization. In fact, this was what impelled me to seek Dr. Cabahug's services as consultant in 2010 to help and guide one of my companies that was then in the throes of uncertainty due to changes in leadership and the departure of some key personnel.

The company's board of directors needed guidance in better understanding and knowing the key people who had stayed on to continue managing the corporation, particularly the middle managers and crucial line personnel. We needed to determine to whom we would entrust leadership roles, and we needed to know as well the short-term and long-term plans of those who had chosen to remain in the company's employ.

Dr. Cabahug initiated an Organization Development (OD) intervention to help the company get through that crisis. That intervention redirected our efforts and gave our organization the proper perspective for achieving our common objective: *success in the business*. As our consultant, Dr. Cabahug immersed himself in our company by staying with our employees full-time on many occasions, working and dining with them, even joining their sports activities to establish a deeper personal relationship with them and to know each one's character and potential much better.

With Dr. Cabahug's expertise in interpersonal relationships and business management, he accomplished with commendable success all of the goals and objectives of his two-month engagement with our company. His OD recommendations properly equipped our core managers and employees with confidence in hurdling the various organizational obstacles that had come our way.

Our company just recently celebrated our 24th anniversary, and 2020 is proving to be a particularly challenging year for us as it is for most businesses everywhere, but our company is fortunate and grateful that it is able to ride through these tough times. The learnings and interventions initiated over a decade ago by Dr. Cabahug are definitely contributing in great measure to our company's resiliency.

With the close friendship that developed between Dr. Cabahug and me during his consultancy engagement with the company, I knew even then that he had long been planning to pen this book of his, *Pathways to Achieving Your Fullest Potential*. It's about time he did, for now Dr. Cabahug can finally share his expertise, mind, and heart with all those who need guidance in human resource development—students, young professionals, human resources practitioners like himself, entrepreneurs, managers, and business leaders.

As a businessman, I am truly delighted to welcome the publication of this highly instructive and motivating book by Dr. Cabahug. Without any doubt in my mind, it would prove to be a very valuable instrument of learning, a useful self-help reference, and an inspiring guide for all people aiming for success in their chosen careers or callings.

ALFRITO D. MAH
President & CEO, Patient Care Corporation
and MRL Ventures, Inc.
President, Northbreeze Development Corp.
   and City Lakeside Development Corp.
Chief Operating Officer, MRL Cybertec Corp.
   and Fil-Anaserve, Inc.
October 2, 2020

PREFACE

Sometime during my studies for a B.S in Commerce in the early 1980s, I developed a strong interest in writing a college textbook about human resource management. The desire to write that book grew and grew over the ensuing years. However, long after graduating from college, after working for many years in academe and in the corporate world, and even after getting a master's degree in Business Management and a doctorate in Human Resources Management, I remained trapped in my professional comfort zone and never found time to write that book.

Then in 2014, after almost 33 years of wallowing in self-doubt and just enjoying short-lived diversions, I finally did something right to make that dream of mine come true—I resigned as business management lecturer from the Bahrain Training Institute under the Kingdom of Bahrain's Ministry of Education, almost 25,000 miles from my homeland the Philippines. Once and for all I decided that it would be such a meaningful and life-changing undertaking for me to share my professional expertise and life experiences through a self-help, self-transformation book that could touch and help improve the lives and careers of others, particularly my fellow Filipinos.

The outcome of that decision that I took as an overseas foreign professional is this book, *Pathways to Achieving Your Fullest Potential*. I believe that on top of classroom teaching and face-to-face consultancy, I have found the perfect platform for sharing a wealth of actionable and tried-and-tested ways to attain greater self-confidence and trust in one's ability to climb the success ladder in today's chaotic world and fast-changing workplaces.

In sharing this book's prescriptions and caveats to those seeking success, I am truly confident that they can make a great difference and positive impact in their lives and careers as they did in mine. I have no doubt that readers of this book who take its self-development pathways to heart can attain that highest goal to pursue in life, which is to become not only a much better version but the best possible version of themselves.

[Sig.]
ARTEMIO B. CABAHUG, DM
Doctor in Management (DM-HRM)
Lapu-Lapu City, Philippines
October __, 2020

OVERVIEW

Like it or not, challenges big and small can get in the way in your life's journeys. When they do, you just have to wrestle with each of those challenges the best you can so you can continue your journey to your intended destination.

It's very important to keep in mind that a trip is rarely the same as a journey. A trip is largely predictable and uneventful; often with no hitch at all, you can just relax or sleep blissfully on board a bus, train, or plane en-route to your destination. In contrast, a journey can turn out to be exciting, challenging, infuriating, tiresome, or terrifying—even all of these simultaneously—because a journey generally takes much longer than a trip and can be occasioned by any number of surprises, of changes of plans, of unpredictable detours, breakdowns, and stoppages. Indeed, if you aren't adequately prepared for a long journey, expect the unexpected to give you not only terrible frustration and physical discomfort but emotional and mental anguish as well.

So this early, you need to ask yourself this question: "When is the right time to start my life's journey?"

Imagine yourself stopping at a major city intersection because as what typically happens in real life, you've realized too late that you still don't know which road is the right road to take for your intended destination. You also may not know the precise time to start the journey, for unlike regular trips that you take from day to day, a journey can involve so many imponderables and unpredictables. That right time to start can be now or anytime at all, so it would be unwise and impracticable for you to mark the precise moment that you think you'd feel most comfortable to begin your journey. When that right moment comes, as that familiar footwear ad commands us, "Just do it!"

The big point to firmly keep in mind is that to get your life journey started in earnest, you need to first develop a truly positive outlook and to assiduously nurture the seeds of optimism in your mind. You must allow these seeds to grow into seedlings and let these seedlings blossom into healthy plants, getting rid of any weed of negativity that threatens to choke them. Only if you've already done this can you get reasonably assured that your life's journey won't result in failure but in great progress and in an abundant harvest of achievement.

INTRODUCTION

When you have the will to take the first step forward in every task you want to achieve, you'll truly be on your way to your pursuit of a fulfilling, accomplished, and happy life. This is for the simple reason that you absolutely need to take that first step to reach the intended destination of all of your life's journeys.

What makes it difficult for many people to take that first step is their inordinate fear that achieving their goal would be very tedious and difficult, thus tempting them to just remain glued to their comfort zone. The truth is that the human brain is pre-wired to perform mainly routine and simple tasks, such that not a few of us don't ever bother or get to see the gold mine just waiting to be tapped inside ourselves. Indeed, we are at a certain level programmed for mediocrity, strongly predisposed to forgetting that what really matters in the journey isn't about where we begin but where we end up and how far it is now from where we started.

Both secular science and the Scriptures themselves tell us that all of humankind are created from dust and will thereafter return to dust, in the same manner that all animals and all forms of vegetation grow out of the soil and thereafter die in the soil. This being clearly evident as the end of all forms of life, however, isn't it a wonder that most of us remain afraid of dirt— deathly afraid of it and of going back to it when, in fact, dirt is a vital component of the soil from where all life begins and ultimately ends?

But not to dwell further on the metaphysical, have you ever contemplated that your purpose in life is figuratively a journey of a thousand miles, and that no matter how long that journey might be, there's virtually no short cut to your intended destination? There's a very practical and obvious reason for this, for once you miss the basic first step, you'll begin to needlessly travel in circles. Looking for the right road to take in such situations becomes practically impossible because when you're just spinning round and round and round, you won't be able to see clearly any road ahead of you.

This is why the best approach to start your life journeyis to know your intended direction first and foremost, and then to take only one step at a time towards the path that you've carefully planned. And you should take that first step without waiting for tomorrow—get rid of that *mañana* habit now!—because in real-world terms, tomorrow is today and waiting for tomorrow is already too late to start your life's journey. Remember that every day always presents a second chance, and to take full advantage of that second chance, you need to decide to do the needed action today, right at the very moment when that second chance presents itself.

Let me now ask you two very crucial questions:

Are you doing the things you want to do because they are part of your real purpose in life?

And if you've failed many times in your pursuit of that purpose, would you allow adversity and hindrance to lead you by the nose to just anywhere or steer away from them and remain steadfast in pursuing your life purpose the best way you see fit?

If your answer to both questions is "yes," it's clear that you haven't discovered yet the vast trove of potential for achievement in your life. You ought to discover and start using those strengths of yours now before it gets too late to do so!

If you stop pursuing your aspirations and dreams in life because you are terrified by all sorts of obstacles, whether real or imagined, all you'd see ahead of you is a road littered with nails and thorns no matter how easy your life's goal might be. When you're blinded by anxiety and fear, there will hardly be any way for you to move forward. Your life can forever remain a listless shadow in the wilderness.

Always remember that dreams are free but the hustle needed to pursue them is sold separately. To uncover the boundless potential that resides within you, you shouldn't allow yourself to be intimidated from travelling the path you've decided to take. Otherwise, you'll be like a weary bird inside a cage that has been left hanging up a tree for so long that when the cage is finally sprung open, the bird can't fly out to freedom because it no longer remembers how to flap its wings.

Take a look at yourself right now: Are you sure that you are capable of flapping your wings so you can soar as high as you possibly can? If you aren't, then how trivial and boring your life must be, with so little motivation or inclination to succeed in anything! Sadly, you've made the grievous mistake of settling for less in your life despite the loads of precious gems inside of you just waiting to be discovered and put to good use.

The color of your landscape will become much brighter once you begin to pursue without letup the things you love to do in life. The pursuit will surely change your life for the better, so don't ever get yourself immobilized by fear of failure. Approach every obstacle and every challenge with a positive and open mind. And don't let barriers stop your journey; instead, always do your utmost to hurdle them.

By deftly maneuvering through any roadblock to your chosen destination, you'll greatly improve your chances of achieving your life goals. But if you just sit idly on the road and wait for that lucky charm or that lucky break, success would never come and would always elude you. You'd be like those misguided souls who just wait for the sun to set every day until their misery ends when they are already buried six feet in the ground.

Of course there will be times when you'd fall into the rut of doubting your talents and abilities, making you think that you aren't good enough to realize your dreams. You must resolutely conquer and cast away those doubts! Remember to look at failure as just a tentative first step to success—that it simply presents an opportunity for you to learn to do things differently the next time around. The fact is that failure is an essential component of life, one that prompts us to undertake the innovations and improvements we need to get over the Mt. Everest that's getting in the way of our success.

It's true that failure has a way of whispering negativity into our ears, insidiously threatening us with the idea that we can never ever achieve what we want in life. When you experience failure personally, it's really very difficult to argue with the whispers you'll hear because the voice is actually your very own. Still, the best way to muffle or suppress that voice is to transform your negative thoughts into positive thoughts— thoughts to enable you to absorb and learn valuable lessons from your ineffective or ineffectual actions in the past.

After all, failure is simply a huge telescope that should guide and not hinder you from navigating your journey into the right direction. Indeed, when you cultivate a positive mind, you'll begin to see your failure not as an insurmountable barrier but as another chance and much-welcome opportunity to advance your life.

Pathways to Achieving Your Fullest Potential

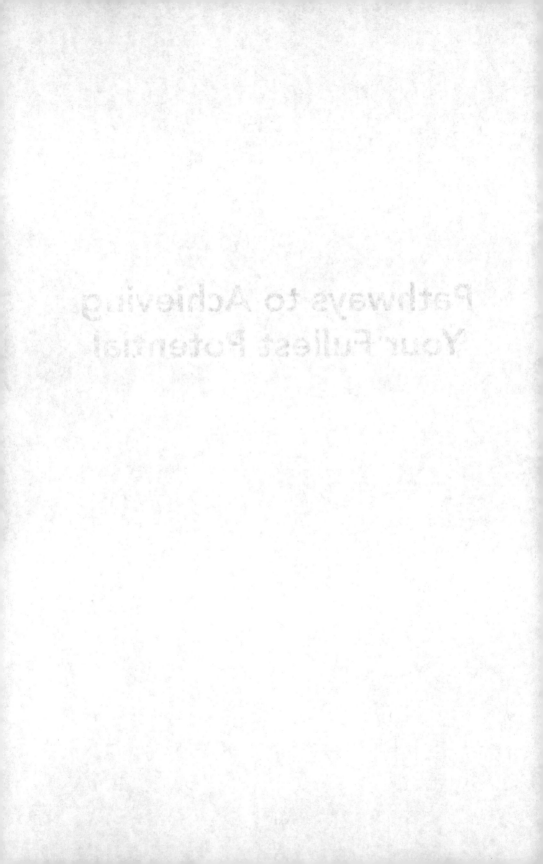

CHAPTER 1

Discovering Your Fullest Potential

"The will to win, the desire to succeed, the urge to reach your full potential... these are the keys that will unlock the door to personal excellence."
—Confucius, Chinese philosopher and politician (551 BC–479 BC)

Have you ever experienced doing something quite well and people told you to keep on doing it because you clearly have the potential to excel in it? If so, the experience must have raised your self-worth, didn't it?

I distinctly remember a college event at the University of Cebu in Cebu City sometime in 2006 when a newly-hired corporate staffer from a private organization—let's just identify him here as Mr. Felix C. to respect his privacy—delivered before an audience of seasoned faculty members what I felt was an outstanding speech. He held me spellbound because I found him much more articulate and engaging than most of our school's faculty members, not even excluding myself who was a relative newcomer at the time.

Right after he left the rostrum, I heartily congratulated Mr. Felix C. Only a little bit flustered by my compliment, he told me that he was just a last-minute replacement for his boss, admitting that he was actually so nervous while delivering his remarks because he said he wasn't really accustomed to speaking in front of audiences.

But no matter his expression of humility, I told myself, "Wow, what a remarkable public display of inner potential! "In retrospect, though, I just didn't know whether he was aware of the public speaking genius that was clearly inside of him.

My point in telling you this anecdote is that if you truly want to know what's missing in you that can give your life great fulfillment and happiness, there's really no need to look for it outside of you. When

1

you do an honest and dispassionate self-appraisal, you'll likely discover that your potential for doing some tasks remarkably well already resides in you.

What this means is that you can't be good by just trying very hard to be good but by finding the inherent goodness that's already built-in within you. All you need is, as I have just mentioned above, your willingness to pursue that serious self-examination into your inner life. You absolutely need to do it to get a better understanding of yourself and be able to discard your limiting beliefs that prevent you from becoming the better person that you want to be. Once you discover and start tapping your inner potentials, you'll find it much easier to propel yourself to become a bigger and more accomplished person than what you are right now.

American motivational speaker Leslie Calvin Brown, who's also a writer and former television host, once said, "Most people fail in life not because they aim high and miss, but because they aim too low and hit."

With that quip, of course, Leslie Brown himself did aim high yet succeeded in hitting the heart of the matter for not a few of us, didn't he? Still, I'd like to give my own take here to amplify that insight of his about success and failure.

Yes, quite a lot of people often fail because they aim too low. But when they realize that they'd always miss targets that are set too high, they'd develop a very strong tendency to keep on setting their targets too low because it's the easiest and surest way to hit those targets without exerting much effort. This is how unaccomplished people can boast to have achieved something consequential in their life even if they had never left their comfort zone in pursuing it.

To hit progressively higher and more difficult targets, of course, requires a sufficiently developed combination of knowledge, abilities, and skills. But that goal isn't really not daunting as it sounds! For by making the most of the natural talents that we already have and by consistently honing and improving them to higher levels, we can all develop the ability to hit any reasonably achievable target that's presented to us.

How about you in particular? Are you aiming at something more challenging and exciting that you really want to achieve? I must say you are because, well, you are reading this self-help, self-improvement book.

To really get your life's journey started in earnest, however, you need to do these five crucial steps now:

1. Clearly understand your life's purpose;
2. Know precisely where you are at this very moment;
3. Decide on exactly who or what you want to become at the end of your journey;
4. Identify the actions you need to take to successfully reach your destination and life goals; and
5. Make a realistic, doable timetable for achieving your action plans.

Sadly, many individuals entertain the notion that their talents and skills are so piddling and so limited that they'd be inadequate for the pursuit of their life goals. It's sad to say that such people, even if they can get themselves started on that pursuit, are tragic failures in the making.

The fact is that if you focus more on bewailing your inadequacies rather than developing your innate wealth of skills, talent, and ability, then whatever inner genius you might have will soon burst and disappear like a bubble in thin air. If you are keenly aware that you lack the skills and knowledge needed for reaching your peak performance but don't do anything to correct those inadequacies, what will happen is that you'll admit defeat sooner or later. You'll simply roll back to that state of mind that's commonly called "poverty mentality."

Social scientists define "poverty mentality" as a way of thinking characterized by an "I can't do" attitude. This way of thinking is said to cause the perpetuation of poverty because the individual's focus is on what he or she doesn't have rather than what he or she does have. People with poverty mentality see themselves as victims in a cruel world and don't believe that anything is ever going to change.

Very often, people just can't will themselves to do an important task or to work on something that they can see is too difficult to accomplish, even if it's a crucial next step for the attainment of their career prospects or long-term goals. As I earlier recounted—I think "confessed" is the more accurate word—in the preface to this book that you're reading now, my dream in college to write it stayed in deep-freeze for almost 33 years. It took me longer than the time it took me to get the educational credentials and work experience that enabled me to become a human resources consultant both in my home country and overseas, and—on a more personal note—get married, raise a family, and put up several business start-ups of my own (more about them later in this book).

What happened was that I committed this classic, all-too-human mistake: waiting too long for that magical moment when you'd feel you're finally in the mood to write the book that you've long dreamed of writing. But the truth is that every time I felt I thought I was getting in that mood to write, I'd lose the nerve and back out, then get right back to my old comfort zone of not even thinking about writing the book at all. This went on and on until mid-2014 when, while in the Middle East as a business management lecturer at the Bahrain Training Institute, I finally decided to quit my job, flew out of the oil-rich kingdom in the Persian Gulf back to the Philippines, then headed back home to Lapu-Lapu City to start writing this book.

But I must say that there's one totally unexpected bonus that I learned from that experience in procrastination: a clear understanding of the very strong correlation between our personal perception of time and how our emotions, actions, and reactions are shaped by it.

Let me try to explain that point:

The dictionary definition of "time" is, of course, *duration*—the measured or measurable period during which an action, process, or condition begins, continues, and ends. On the other hand, "emotion" is defined as a conscious mental reaction that's experienced subjectively, one that's usually directed toward a specific object and is often accompanied by physiological and behavioral changes in the individual.

Time is therefore not only our instinctive way of synchronizing our every action, emotion, and reaction with the ticking of the clock but also a relentless taskmaster that goads us to do whatever we want or need to do at any moment in our life.

Can you imagine how disastrous it would be if time—yes, time itself!—suddenly and inexplicably careens to a stop while you're doing a great pitch for yourself to a prospective employer, one that could land you a very important life-changing job? Time coming to a stop would be nothing less than an end-of-the-world experience for you and for anyone!

For productive or success-oriented individuals then, time is a unique, very precious, and irreplaceable resource that they won't ever waste or dissipate with needless actions or emotions. There may always be a lot of time for you and me and everybody else for that matter, but once we lose or waste our own time, it's gone forever and there's absolutely no way we can ever recover it.

This being the case, we must be emotionally prepared to accomplish all of our must-do's today no matter how difficult or complicated they might be. Only then can we be sure that things will run smoothly for us in doing our next tasks tomorrow and the next.

Precisely how do you do that in your particular case? Begin by trying to understand yourself much better—your strengths, your inherent limitations, your predispositions. Make a firm personal resolve to control your emotions when under great stress, distress, or duress. And more important for the long term, work hard to rewire your mindset to be truly competitive.

Clearly recognize the fact that in many ways, your brain makes you very much like a businessman or woman engaged in computer software sales. You won't prosper or survive long in that business if you don't upgrade your software offerings as often and as soon as the manufacturers come up with upgrades for their products. Because of the cutthroat competition in the software industry, your competitors who are first to carry every new software or new upgrade will run you out of business in no time at all!

As soon as you discover your strong potential for success in a particular undertaking, firmly resolve to continually develop and grow that potential. Don't expect that potential to grow overnight nor to grow by itself like magic.

Most children normally dream of owning something precious or beautiful or fantastic—anything at all they can imagine—that will make them the envy of other children. Not much later they would dream of perhaps becoming a big somebody in the not-so-distant future, like a Mark Zuckerberg or a Jeff Bezos or a J.K. Rowling or an Oprah Winfrey depending on their respective aptitudes and intended career paths.

When you recall the many wondrous worldly acquisitions or role models you yourself must have dreamed of when you were still a child, you'll likely burst into embarrassed giggles when you realize that they were all so grand and pompous and unrealistic and, well, attainable only by a very wide stretch!

As young people get on in years, of course, reality bites as they say. They begin to see that to really achieve their aspirations in life, they should be more specific or realistic in setting their goals, their targets, their aspirations, and their yearnings for success. This is because soon enough, they'll form the core and driving force of their purpose in life.

If you have a passion for a particular sport or hobby, for example, you'd try your best to excel in it. In my case, as a 12-year-old I was already a member of a softball junior team created by my Dad, the late Alberto Cabahug. The sport was introduced to us by the American military personnel assigned at Mactan Air Base in Lapu-Lapu City in the early 1970s; most of them played excellent softball and my Dad, who was a local businessman, took to the sport like fish to the water. My father had many friends among the Mactan Air Base military and civilian personnel.

We called our softball team the Mactan Goldies, and it soon became a formidable fighting team that won numerous championship games in Lapu-Lapu City where the Cabahug family was residing at that time.

In high school, however, my focus in sports shifted, first to martial arts and later to basketball. I gravitated towards basketball because most of our relatives were basketball varsity players; in fact, I even had a relative, Elmer Cabahug, who played for the PureFoods team in the Philippine Basketball Association.

Upon graduation from college, I got addicted to playing lawn tennis, which became one of my best forms of exercise. Until today, I still play competitive tennis. I find playing it very enjoyable, for it's a sport that you can continue to play even during your senior years and even long after your retirement.

CHAPTER 2

How to Design Your Own Life

"If you plan on being anything less than you are capable of being, you will probably be unhappy all the days of your life."—**Abraham Harold Maslow, American psychologist (1908 – 1970)**

As individuals in civilized society, we all find ourselves searching for meaning and purpose in our lives. But why does life have to be like this? It's obviously because without exception, each of us aspires to attain a happier, more abundant, and more fulfilling life—a life that would bring us to a world that's shaped largely by our own selves and our own exertions.

How you'll be able to design your life will greatly depend on the way your own persona has been molded and developed from childhood to adulthood. You are what you are today because of many factors: your surroundings, the things that happened to you as you grew up, your failures and successes, your education, and, of course, the people around your life—your parents, your siblings, your relatives, your friends, your teachers. All of them have influenced and contributed in shaping who and what you are today.

Now imagine seeing a house that's truly beautiful. Such a house obviously didn't happen simply by chance. It could only have been built based on an excellent design by a competent architect. And that architect must have come up with the design following the specific preferences of a discerning client based on an agreed-upon house construction budget.

If that architect was able to design such a magnificent house, then there's no reason why you can't make as splendid a blueprint for your own life. The design for the ideal life you are aspiring for will largely be of your own choosing. You yourself are the architect, and you're the only one who's calling the shots on how your life should turn out and look like. In sum, what's in your drawing board today is your own life, your own plan, your own initiative.

But don't get the idea that designing your life would be easy. It definitely won't be a walk in the park, so to speak. This is because it's a continuing process, an undertaking that can entail a lot of modifications and—to be truly candid about it— a lot of trial and error besides.

When designing your life, a key question you'll need to ask yourself is this: "Am I living a life of my own design or is it one largely imposed by societal pressure?"

All throughout your life's journey, in fact, your life's design will remain a work in progress. Along the way, you'll need to add what you discover is missing from its design. You'll have to discard what you found you don't really need or what you no longer need because of unavoidable circumstances or unexpected developments in your life.

Many people believe in the power of dreams and of their subconscious to influence the direction of their life's journeys. In fact, you must have noticed that both the popular and scientific literature have lots of stories, some authentic and others perhaps apocryphal, about the power of dreams to trigger important or revolutionary ideas later in the dreamer's life.

My perennial favorites are two interesting anecdotes about how the Theory of Relativity originated from two dreams of Albert Einstein when he was still a young man. As most of us already know, Einstein was awarded the Nobel Prize in Physics in 1921 (he received it one year later in 1922) for his outstanding contributions to theoretical physics, particularly for his discovery of the law of the photoelectric effect.

Einstein himself described one of his dreams, which he recalled happened in the 1890s when he was between 11 and 16 years of age. In his own words, "I was sledding with my friends at night. I started to slide down the hill but my sled started going faster and faster. I was going so fast that I realized I was approaching the speed of light. I looked up at that point and I saw the stars. They were being refracted into colors I had never seen before. I was filled with a sense of awe.

I understood in some way that I was looking at the most important meaning in my life."

In retrospect, Einstein put it on record that his entire scientific career was a meditation on this particular dream.

Another often-told story of the origins of the Theory of Relativity was Einstein's pastoral dream of a jumping herd of cows in the Alpine mountains when he was still a child. In that dream, according to a 2018 online *Reader's Digest* feature collection entitled "13 World-Changing Ideas That Came from Dreams (Literally)," young Albert was walking alongside a stream when he noticed a small herd of cows huddling near an electric fence. Some of the cows were calmly munching on grass with their heads slipped through the fence slats.

When Einstein out of curiosity approached the cows, a farmer who was fiddling with a car battery came into view. The farmer mischievously connected battery to the fence and the surge of electricity made all of the cows jump back in terror.

From Einstein's perspective, the cows jumped into the air all at once—simultaneously—and scampered in unison into safety. The farmer violently disagreed with Einstein though, insisting that the cows jumped to the air one by one—meaning only one at a time—they fled from the scene helter-skelter.

What followed was a prolonged and unresolved dispute between the young Einstein and the farmer over their differing perceptions of the same reflex movements of the cows. This dream has been claimed in some accounts to be the precursor to the scientific theory that Einstein came up with much later in life. The theory postulated that depending on their unique vantage points, observers can experience time and space in vastly different ways.

In presenting these two anecdotes about dreams that presaged remarkable achievements, I'm not saying that you must wait for a dream in your sleep to figure out a design of your own life. My point is that if it's possible for some people to create their life design in their subconscious, you definitely can build your own destiny even better with your conscious mind—that is, when you're fully awake.

We can all have both conscious and subconscious dreams in our life, and we should never allow any circumstance to destroy our fondest dreams because the moment those dreams die, our life could become like a broken-winged bird that forever can no longer fly.

When you allow other people to dictate the tempo of your life, someday you'll find yourself taking the path they themselves always take, and your own chosen path will become a footprint in the sand that will soon be erased by the wind. Worse, if you become a victim of public opinion and allow the thoughts of the crowd to dominate your mind, you'll soon live a life that's not your own but that of faceless others.

So it's always better to live a life of your own choice, to become the best manifestation of yourself in everything you do. When you yourself devise the blueprint of your path for your intended life journeys, it becomes your own path. It's yours alone. Others may walk that path with you, but nobody can walk that path for you.

We are all born and blessed with our own unique talents, our own convictions, our own beliefs, and our own aspirations in life. Our Creator firmly guides us to the right path to follow, making sure that we are not so easily knocked off the track; the only thing we need to do is to use our good judgment, to make the right choices in life, and to establish a strong belief in ourselves. Indeed, if we don't believe strongly enough in our own inner genius to overcome life's adversities, then our life would become a hollow shell, anemic of color and anemic of meaning as well.

Sometimes, after winning some tough struggles in life, you can become so complacent as to forget your bigger goal of reaching our highest aspirations in life. You can become too comfortable and to rest or bask too long on the laurels of our recent accomplishments. But this return to your comfort zone can only give you temporary joy; in fact, it will only waste the valuable time you need for your pursuit of your true worth.

Embracing temporary comforts can lead you to the vicious cycle of doing the same easy and routine actions in your life over and over again. When this happens, your great potential for human growth will be compromised. It will become insufferably difficult for you to succeed and accomplish your purpose in life.

Let me now discuss how to achieve your growth the best you can in your life.

Human growth consists of three stages:

1. **The "Me" Stage**– the egocentric stage (You are self-centered);
2. **The "Us" Stage**– the ethnocentric stage (You are evaluative of others according to your own standards); and
3. The "All of us" Stage– the worldcentric stage (You desire the best for all people and all living beings).

In which of these three stages do you find yourself right now? And which of them do you finally want to reach or achieve?

Of course the third stage—the "All of us" stage—is the ideal and most desirable choice for anyone. For if your wish and everyone else's are for the greater good of everybody, then the whole world would be an optimally better place to live for everyone. There will be harmony among all of the people everywhere.

Have you ever experienced successfully reaching a big goal that you had set for yourself and yet you still felt empty and unfulfilled after all of your efforts to reach that goal? It's most likely because you decided to go after that goal without first fully understanding yourself, without first knowing where you are now, and without first recognizing what it is really that you want for your life in the future.

Always keep on mind that your goal is not the same as your life's purpose. For instance, when you say, "I want to be a popular heart surgeon when I finish school,"you are setting a goal for yourself; but when you envision yourself to be of help to others whether you become a doctor or not, then that's your life's purpose.

The difference is that your goal is a specific plan that you'll endeavor to reach, but your life's purpose is your mission statement—the very reason for why you exist in this world.

Have you ever observed a salesman who gets to sell his merchandise to a customer only because the impatient customer just wants to avoid the litany of his sales talk? If you were that loquacious salesman, you've achieved your goal, but your customer didn't get the true value of the item you were able to sell to him.

Remember that unlike your goals, your life's purpose is an ongoing process and not a destination. Indeed, your life's purpose involves tons of constant self-process and self-resolution. When you don't have the motivation to do anything or everything in your life, it's likely because you still don't know or still haven't found your definite purpose in life.

Take as example a highly-paid company employee with a good job who doesn't show any passion or enthusiasm in his work. The reason for that could be anything. Perhaps the work is a mismatch to his skills and talent, maybe his boss has such a hateful and demotivating bad temper, or the whole workplace itself is largely staffed with unenergetic nonperformers.

If you're the type who looks at his job as simply to punch the Bundy clock at 8:00 A.M. and do the same at 5:00 P.M. and then just look forward to paydays and weekends, then you're obviously stepping on the wrong accelerator to move your life forward. You definitely can't reasonably expect to make your mark in this world. Because for that to happen, you need to be engaged in something that truly has a significant value to you; you must be able to change your mindset and act more purposively.

From Steve Pavlina, an American self-help author and motivational speaker who wrote the book *Personal Development for Smart People*, I learned a lot about the concept of life alignment.

Essentially, this is how he described this visioning technique: "Alignment comes down to working on these four questions until they all produce the same answer:

1. **What do you want to do?** This is your "desire."
2. **What can you do?** This is your "ability."
3. **What should you do?** This is your "purpose."
4. **What must you do?** This is your "need."

One very valuable lesson Pavlina shares in his book is that sometimes, while searching for our true identity, we may discover that we have a weakness in a particular aspect of our life—aspects in which our life, for one reason or another, doesn't align with our personal values.

In your workplace, for example, you might be highly valued by your company for your ability to communicate effectively and it's the main reason why you've been assigned as a company trainer. All of a sudden, however, top management decides to permanently transfer you to Accounting because your boss somehow found out that you have a knack for numbers.

However, you might feel that working with numbers isn't aligned with your current career goals, so now you have a major dilemma—to decline the transfer to Accounting and ask to be retained in your current job in communication, and if the company decides to transfer you to Accounting anyway, for you to look for another job closer to your heart at the earliest possible time.

Problems with life alignment can be even broader and more serious when it involves the whole of the organization instead.

In 2010, as a human resources consultant for a big company in Metro Manila, I was asked to conduct organizational development (OD) for the entire organization. My findings: a dismal failure of leadership; crumbling interpersonal relationship among department heads and their staff; lack of coordination and unity among managers and subordinates; avoidance of responsibility and accountability; factionalism; distrust and disrespect.

The bottom line of those findings: serious misalignment of the values of the higher and middle managers and the rank-and-file personnel with the organization's mission and vision.

My point here is that you couldn't stir an organization into the right direction when its members are moving in various disparate directions, in the same manner that you'd be unable to reach your desired life goals if you are misdirected and don't understand early enough the real meaning and purpose of your life.

In my own professional life, I've experienced many days of working 12 hours or more non-stop, yet time just flew like a pleasant breeze because I really loved what I was doing. There were times, however, when it felt like forever after working for just two hours on a particularly unchallenging piece of work, making me almost run amok just to get it done. I'm sure many of you have also experienced similar situations in your career.

Keep in mind that when you're working just for the money, you won't last long in the job; you'd soon get tired and unhappy doing what you're doing. If you work from the heart with true passion, however, you'd thrive and take delight in your work and you won't be counting the hours until it's done.

The impact of life alignment in human growth and performance applies to every line of work or personal pursuit. Outside of your regular work, perhaps you enjoy giving free computer programming tutorials, maybe you love being a community development volunteer, or you probably excel and love to compete in a particular sport. The desires of your heart will enable you to pursue them with vigor and enthusiasm. In all cases, the point is to discover what you love doing and to do it with passion as if there's no tomorrow.

A major feature of creating one's life blueprint is called "visioning."

Visioning is developing a specific plan or goal for your future. To create a clear achievable goal for yourself, however, you need to first sit down, relax, then imagine the future by bringing it to the present. That's what visioning is. It's a very effective way to foresee and understand what you really want to do with your life.

When I was still working as middle management staff early in my professional career, I'd regularly set my goals through visioning. First, I'd go to a quiet place alone to meditate. This personal ritual gave me the state of mind to personally "visit" the future, to see myself in that future, then bring to the present what I see of myself in that future.

Such planned visioning is undertaken by most of the successful individuals and leaders we read about today. They'd look at the future through today's mirror to make their goals crystal clear, giving them the vision, motivation, and inspiration to follow through, and then to pursue their goals with the right moves that need to be taken on the way to that desired future.

One remarkable example of an individual who used the power of visualization to attain great success is Hollywood actor Jim Carrey.

In the early 1990s, Carrey was an unknown actor struggling to just get by. To keep himself motivated, he decided to write himself a check for $10 million for "acting services rendered," dated it for the year 1994, and carried it in his wallet to provide him daily inspiration.

Precisely in the year 1994 that he had postdated that dream, Carrey learned he had reaped exactly $10 million for his role in the movie *Dumb and Dumber*, a comedy about two good-hearted but completely pathetic, dumb, and hopeless guys who do nothing but make complete fools of themselves until they stumble upon a briefcase of a mobster boss full of money. In that movie, Carrey form a duo with fellow comedian Jeff Daniels and both gave great and memorable performances.

The film grossed $247 million at the box office, developed a huge cult following in the years since its release, and solidified Carrey's reputation as one of the most prominent actors of the 1990s.

Another visionary person who made himself big-time in the world in so many astounding ways is Arnold Schwarzenegger.

As we all know, the former Austrian-American professional bodybuilder—he began lifting weights at age 13—won the Mr. Universe title at age 20 and later won the Mr. Olympia contest seven times. He later gained worldwide fame as a Hollywood film actor for his breakthrough role in the box-office-hit film *Conan the Barbarian* (1982), and he solidified his movie success as the title character in the phenomenally successful science-fiction action film series *The Terminator* (1984).

In 2003, Schwarzenegger left acting when he was elected as California's state governor in a special recall election to replace the incumbent governor. He was reelected as the 2006 California governor to serve a full term, completing his second term as governor in 2011 before going back to movie acting.

Schwarzenegger swore by the power of visualization to reach his body-building goals and his eventual success in politics and business: "I had this fixed idea of growing a body like Reg Park who was a popular English bodybuilder and won Mr. Universe in 1951, 1958 and 1965.

The model was there in my mind; I only had to grow enough to fill it. The more I focused in on this image and worked and grew, the more I saw it was real and possible for me to be like him."

Later, when he transitioned to his careers in acting and politics, Schwarzenegger said he employed similar mental tricks: "It's the same process I used in bodybuilding. What you do is create a vision of who you want to be—and then live that picture as if it were already true."

CHAPTER 3

Create Your Personal Goals for Your Life

> *"What you get by achieving your goals is not as important as what you become when you achieve your goals."—Zig Ziglar, American author, salesman, and motivational speaker (1926–2012)*

Can you still remember the conversation between Alice and the Cheshire Cat in Lewis Carroll's 1865 fantasy novel, *Alice's Adventures in Wonderland?*

Here's that conversation in the novel:

Alice: Would you tell me, please, which way I ought to go from here?

The Cheshire Cat: That depends a good deal on where you want to get to.

Alice: I don't much care where.

The Cheshire Cat: Then, it doesn't much matter which way you go.

Alice: ...So long as I get somewhere.

The Cheshire Cat: Oh, you're sure to do that, if only you walk long enough.

The lesson from that conversation is, of course, that if you insist to travel in an unknown path, you'll be like a ship without a navigation system drifting into a dark, deep, and unknown ocean.

Indeed, if you don't plan at all where you are going, you'll be traveling just any path, always crossing your fingers that somehow you'll arrive at some destination. It will be like driving across the vast Sahara Desert alone in a Nissan or Toyota hatchback when suddenly a very violent sandstorm blows, rendering zero visibility to everything around

17

you. You have no contingency plan, no mobile phone, no provisions for anything, so you get hopelessly lost and desperate shrouded by the swirling darkness.

The moral of that Lewis Carroll parable is a timeless and universal: You can't just start your journey with neither a clear plan nor a definite direction. Its essence is likewise vividly captured by this Japanese proverb that's often quoted and sometimes attributed to Soichiro Honda, the Japanese engineer and industrialist who established Honda Motors to great success: "Vision without action is a daydream. Action without vision is a nightmare."

So you must always prepare a concrete plan for your goal, for without a plan, your goal becomes just wishful thinking that's sure to fail. To fulfill your dreams in life, to paraphrase another Japanese saying, you should become a goal digger who always goes and digs deeper and deeper.

When creating your life goals, make sure that they come from a genuine longing in your heart. Your goals will then be much stronger, more durable, and not just wishy-washy ones that would get crushed into pieces by negative external forces in your life.

Those forces could be in the form of small and big pressures exerted on your person by your family, your colleagues, your friends, and likewise by the enticements of social media and by the blandishments of TV or radio advertising and talk shows. Any of them can trick your brain and make you take action or covet things that go against your true desires in life.

To succeed in your life's journeys, it's very important for you to clearly know and fully internalize the difference between your goals, your mission, and your vision.

Your goals are the things you desire to fulfill in the future; they are the stepping stones to your life's purpose or what's commonly called your personal vision. For instance, when you've long desired to become a famous defense lawyer and you've truly become one, then you've reached that life goal. But what you desire or intend to do when you've reached that goal is what your vision in life is.

When you become a famous defense lawyer whose services are

sought after by society's high and mighty, that vision of yours could be to amass wealth huge enough for you to afford a big mansion in your city's millionaire's row and a first-rate education for your children in foreign universities. That, clearly, is not a very noble vision because it's for your own selfish interest and personal aggrandizement.

In contrast, you could envision yourself as a magnanimous wealthy philanthropist like Microsoft's Bill Gates; like him, you tap the boundless bounty from your legal practice to set up a foundation that provides free legal services and financial assistance to poor, underprivileged litigants in your region or province. This is clearly a selfless humanitarian vision that demonstrates strong social responsibility and a sincere desire to give back to society a substantial part of the blessings it has afforded you.

In short, your vision is who or what you would like to become in the future—it is your greatly wished-for final destination in life. On the other hand, your mission is your reason or justification for why you exist in this world. Without a clear mission in life, your vision for your life's journey will be clouded and success will remain elusive to you.

You'll probably find it surprising, if not outright unbelievable, that in 1986, even if I already had a B.S. in Commerce (major in management) and six months of work experience as project human resource manager of a Makati City-based construction firm assigned to its Tacloban City project, I decided to fly to the Middle East almost 5,000 miles from my hometown of Mandaue in Cebu to work as a contractual laborer.

I had signed up for a two-year contract with a Saudi Arabian firm as a US$210- a-month field worker in an electrification project in the Wadi Dawasir desert, about 375 miles from the city of Riyadh. This was right after I closed down my floundering native handicraft business in Mandaue City, fervently hoping to be able to resume it with funds from my overseas employment.

The position of field worker that I signed up for sounded much better than a construction worker's, but it was in truth that of a manual laborer! However, the project manager who hailed from the same hometown as mine assured me that he'd change my status to administrative staff with better pay after working with him for only three months.

That made it sound like a great and lifesaving deal to me. Still, my friends and relatives urged me not to proceed with that decision to work overseas, and as a lowly laborer at that! They tried with all their might to scare me with the terrors of homesickness, sweltering weather conditions, and the many restrictions to non-Muslim foreigners working in the Middle East.

But those warnings were to no avail. I had made up my mind, and my decision also happened to give me the opportunity to achieve a fond dream of mine—to work abroad and experience working in the Middle East and get paid in U.S. dollars. I wanted to test my fortitude as to whether I could really finish a two-year contract under an extremely hot environment.

My first work assignment—I was assured that it would only be a temporary one—was to work with another Filipino laborer, using a huge jackhammer to drill and dig holes for the electric posts that the company was putting up across the desert. I started working in mid-August, which is the hottest and most unbearable season outdoors in Saudi Arabia.

On the day that my turn came to drive the jackhammer, I got so breathlessly tired after doing it for only a short while. My brain began to swirl with negative thoughts and deep regret over what I was doing. The jackhammer's overpowering vibration shook my body and limbs too much that I felt I was on the brink of disintegrating. The only thing that prevented me from crying out loud in pain and desperation was my fervent goal of finishing my two-year contract.

A few days later, owing to my overpowering exhaustion in the desert heat, I actually fell to the ground with the jackhammer. I nearly passed out. When I got up and came back to my senses, I tried my best to look as if nothing untoward happened. But my Filipino co-worker did see what happened, and I got startled when he started pumping me with probing questions.

He asked me in Tagalog what type of job I held and what work I did back in the Philippines. I lied, telling him with a straight face that I was a construction worker like him.

He didn't believe me. Then he approached me, casually took both of my hands, felt them, and then knowingly said in jest: "No, my friend, you couldn't be a construction worker like me. Unlike mine, your hands have no calluses at all, so I'm sure the only tool you were using back in the Philippines was a ball pen."

All I could do when he said that was to affirm its truth with a pained, embarrassed smile.

The following day, my fellow worker reported my situation to our project manager. I was thereafter transferred to the company's survey team. Later, I got transferred to the main office as computer assistant for the last six months of my contract. I no longer did backbreaking manual work for the rest of my two-year contract.

Did I or do I regret having done manual work in faraway Riyadh that was way below my qualifications and capabilities? No, not at all! I was satisfied and felt fulfilled by the experience, having proved to myself that I was capable of surmounting whatever obstacles I'd encounter or get thrown my way while I am pursuing my life's goals.

Talking about life goals, they come in two types: long-term and short-term.

Keep in mind though that a long-term goal can sometimes be reduced to short-term. Take the need for housing, for example. Your long-term goal may be to own a big house for you and your family, but if you've just started a business venture and you don't have a family of your own yet, you can modify that long-term goal into a short-term goal by first renting a more affordable apartment. Calibrating and recalibrating your major goals according to how your situation in life develops is the best and most optimal way to plan and pursue your life plans.

Once you've set your goal, the next important thing to do is to establish objectives to make your goals doable and achievable. Such objectives are specific shorter-term actions to guide you in reaching your goal; as a rule, objectives are more specific and easier to measure than your goals.

Assume that your goal is to be this year's champion of the World Eskrima Kali Arnis Federation (WEKAF), a 50-country organization formed in Cebu in 1989. It was founded by Supreme Grand Master

Atty. Dionisio Cañete to promote the sporting version of *eskrima* (stickfighting) throughout the world.

Our very own Dexler Bolambao, who won seven golds for Team Philippines in eight different categories, became the overall champion of the 2018 15th WEKAF World championships in Maui, Hawaii. To achieve that objective, Dexler had to win progressively higher-level *eskrima* tournaments in his country of origin and in his adopted country. He had to adapt himself to his new environment in the United States to reach that goal.

If you don't have a clear idea and clear direction for your goals, you'd surely just get lost along the way. So choose goals that truly arouse your passion. Put them in writing along with your specific objectives. Then continually review them until you're definitely sure that they are truly your desired and real purpose in your life.

Formal studies in human development have established that people who wrote down their goals, shared this information with a friend, and sent weekly updates to that friend were on average 33% more successful in accomplishing their stated goals than those who merely formulated goals.

The premise of the study—that people who write down specific goals for their future are far more likely to be successful than those who have either unwritten goals or have no specific goals at all—has inspired the teachings of many self-help authors and personal coaches. Many of them are agreed on this point: If you don't put your goals in writing, they will likely remain merely as wishes.

You can use the acronym "SMART" as an effective, easy-to-remember, and easy-to-monitor guide in creating effective personal and business goals. This is because its five letters can accurately and memorably represent the initials of what many human resource development experts consider to be "good" goal statements.

Take a look at what each letter of SMART stands for:

S for "Specific": S stands for the clarity of your goal. It reminds you of the six W's and one H to consider when considering, developing, and remembering the elements of goal awareness.

The 6Ws are these: "who," "what," "when," "where," "which,"

and "why. And the lone H is: "how." Altogether, all seven S elements comprise the intent or gains of accomplishing the goal.

M is for "Measurable": M means that your purpose is clear, that you can calculate your own growth, that you know where you are going, and that you can see how far you still need to go.

A is for "Attainable": A means that the goal should be doable and achievable; that although it may be difficult, it's not impossible; and that although it isn't easy, you believe it is achievable.

R is for "Realistic": R means that to ensure that your goal is significant, it should be reasonable and consistent with your values in life.

T is for "Timely": T means that the indicated timetable for the outcome is achievable.

Here are examples of SMART goals that you can use as prototypes:

Specific: "I will acquire three new clients for my small management consulting company."

Measurable: "I will quantify my growth by the number of new clients I will get."

Attainable: "I will seek recommendations from my current customers and later publicize some promotional initiative based on the best of them.

Realistic: The more clients I acquire, the more the return on the capital that I invested and thus accelerate progress for my firm."

Timely: "Within a month, I must acquire three to five new clients."

Once you're finished formulating your goal and you're already working on your action plan, use the familiar SAFE goal concept as the end-result of your SMART goal

SAFE is an acronym for the actions needed to appraise and evaluate goals:

- See the end result
- Accept the end result
- Feel the end result
- Express the end result

Objectively, your main focus should be on making a goal "specific."

For instance, assume that you want to improve your tennis skills. Instead of playing just twice a week, you can decide to play every other day, and then play only with players far better than you.

Not only that, you can follow video instructions on how to play better, then experiment on those suggested moves with players below your level to reduce the pressure on you to learn those suggested moves.

Make a firm commitment to yourself to do your daily rituals without letup. This will ensure that you'll stay focused on your specific area of interest and on no other, and avoid getting easily derailed from doing what you need to do.

If you lose focus, you'll procrastinate and become complacent, and complacency is the killer of growth, one that can prevent you from advancing and attaining your goals. Never be complacent if you are determined to accomplish your purpose in life.

On December 22 in the year 2019, I became a victim of my own complacency; I got very lax and got too easily swayed by the allures of social media on my mobile phone. This happened upon my arrival at Los Angeles International Airport at 3:00 P.M. from Hong Kong, and I was queuing up at the assigned gate for my flight to San Antonio, Texas, at 6:56 P.M.

At that point the airport's electronic flight schedule monitor flashed this message: "Boarding in 18 minutes."

When that much time had elapsed, however, the passengers on my queue suddenly dispersed, with none of them going to the designated boarding area. I got rattled by what happened, so I went to the airline staff counter to inquire what the ruckus was all about.

I asked if my boarding pass reflected the correct boarding gate number and was told it did, but I failed to ask why the passengers in my queue had all left and hadn't come back yet to board our flight.

Thinking that my flight was delayed, I calmly walked back, sat on an empty bench, then excitedly started browsing Facebook on my mobile phone. I did that without pause for quite a while and completely lost track of time. When I went back to the counter, I was shocked when the airline staff told me that the plane I was supposed to board had already departed.

She politely asked me to rebook for the next scheduled flight the following day, but in my anger and confusion I messed up with my rebooking, too. The end result was that I stayed at the airport almost 24 hours. After so much listless waiting, I finally got another flight passing through Dallas Airport and arrived at San Antonio, Texas, midnight of December 24 just in time for Christmas!

That was a very heartbreaking lesson that I think I'll never forget. It happened because I became too complacent and allowed myself to be distracted by Facebook on my mobile phone, making me lose my focus and drawing me away from attaining a very important goal. Truth to tell, that experience has made me a firm believer of this breezy, irreverent axiom: *Life is what's happening while you're busy on your mobile phone.*

Still on the same subject of distraction, have you bothered to figure out why horses that draw carriages or carts have both of their eyes half-covered? You haven't yet?

Well, the reason is that with those blinders, a horse can look only straight ahead and don't get distracted unnecessarily. The horse is thus able to trot calmly or run faster to convey the carriage or cart to its intended destination.

Take those blinders away and the horse could get off-kilter or led astray so often by any distracting sight that its eyes latches on en route, thus causing unexpected travel delays to the consternation of the passengers on board the carriage or cart.

CHAPTER 4

Create an Action Plan for Your Goal

"In life, lots of people know what to do, but few
people actually do what they know. Knowing
is not enough! You must take action."
—Anthony Jay Robbins, American author,
coach, motivational speaker, philanthropist
(Born 1960)

Now let's go down to the brass tacks of success, so to speak.

Only when the director who's filming a TV show or movie has shouted "Action!" will the actors and actresses begin to act their respective roles according to the script for that particular scene. This is exactly what needs to happen when you begin your journey of fulfilling your goals in life. But in the real world, of course, that director and the principal actor is you yourself.

So once the action starts you've got to be truly decisive! You can't afford to procrastinate or dillydally. For as is often said, when you get to start the action right on time for your own life's goals and firmly follow through, you've already achieved half of the battle of reaching them. And without any doubt, the key to accomplishing our goals in life is getting those goals acted upon promptly and making the needed follow-throughs with the right moves.

Our life's goals are nothing less than real seeds. After you've sown them and they grow into seedlings, you need to nurture them by chopping off the weeds that can choke them, by consistently watering and fertilizing, and by sheltering them from bad weather and all sorts of pests. Like your nurture for those seedlings, only when you pursue your life's goals with love and care can you expect to harvest success from your undertakings.

Success begins with the building of life goals that are challenging

27

enough, goals that can ignite great enthusiasm and draw a strong and deep personal commitment from you and those who will work with you to achieve them. And make sure that those goals are difficult enough but realistically doable.

If your life goals are too simple and bland and unambitious, they're likely to prove not worth pursuing at all; indeed, you and your associates are likely to lose interest and abandon them in midstream. This is why you should shun goals that underestimate your capability to drive your inner genius; they should be able to strongly engage you on a personal level so no distraction can easily derail you from your path.

Another key element in goal-planning is the setting the goal's timetable. This is the time realistically available for you to achieve it. And once you start pursuing your goal,you need to be sure that you can continue working on it from start to finish. Don't get started on a goal that would be impossible or impracticable for you to achieve within your productive years.

Of course, we can't all be a great prodigy like Bill Gates who, along with Paul Allen, founded Microsoft in 1975 when he was only in his early 20s. Obstacles and complications were many, but Bill Gates had all of 40 years ahead of him to conceptualize, develop, and market the Microsoft Windows operating system.

Through his innovations and unrelenting efforts, however, Microsoft Windows became so reliable, so popular, and so in demand that it had already captured over 90% market share of the world's personal computers by the 1990s.

In contrast, timetable-wise, success was a much tougher nut to crack for Harland David Sanders. As most of us fried-chicken lovers know, Col. Sanders was already past the usual retirement age at 65 when he began producing Kentucky Fried Chicken in 1952 and made it one of the big-time pioneers of modern franchising.

By 1964 or just 12 years thereafter, he had already established a franchised network of over 600 Kentucky Fried Chicken outlets in the United States, Canada, Mexico, England, and Jamaica.

But a swifter, even more remarkable success timetable has been notched by our very own Emmanuel "Manny" Pacquiao in the

Philippines, who until today is regarded as one of the greatest professional boxers of all time.

Coming from an extremely poor family in General Santos City in Mindanao, he dropped out of high school in before he was 10 due to his family's extreme poverty. With martial-artist Bruce Lee and the boxer Muhammad Ali as role models, he took to professional boxing in his hometown in Mindanao as a matter of survival.

In 1998 at age of 19, Manny won his first major World Boxing Council (WBC) title in the flyweight division, and by age of 40 had won a total of four world championships in the flyweight, featherweight, lightweight, and welterweight divisions.

By 2019 he had become a multimillionaire with a reported net worth of $220 million, and was able to parlay his remarkable success as a professional boxer by also winning a six-year term as a senator in his own homeland the Philippines. He's just approaching the age of 42 as of this writing.

Of his hard scrabble early years Pacquiao, known to his million fans worldwide as "PacMan," reminisces: "Many of you know me as a legendary boxer, and I'm proud of that. However, that journey was not always easy. When I was younger, I became a fighter because I had to survive. I had nothing. I had no one to depend on except myself. I realized that boxing was something I was good at, and I trained hard so that I could keep myself and my family alive."

Whatever kind of timetable you're pursuing for your personal and business undertakings, however, it's very important to make timely follow-throughs to ensure that the actions or activities needed to achieve that goal are on track and are properly implemented.

A simple but very effective tool that can help you do this is the SSK Model.

The SSK, an acronym for "Stop Start Keep," is a formal reminder system that prompts us to ask the following questions:

What should I Stop doing? These are the activities or events that didn't go as planned.

What should I Start doing? These are the activities or events that could help but were not performed.

What should I Keep doing? These are the activities or events that were successfully implemented and should therefore be continued.

Once you've come up with a clear goal, you have to draw up a detailed action plan that lists of all the tasks and activities that need to be done to achieve that goal. Both figuratively and literally, consider your action plan as a bright guiding star in the darkness of the night, providing you a firm guide post when the going gets tough so you don't get lost along the way.

It bears repeating at this point that your timetable is a very crucial component of your action plan. Without a specific time-frame for executing the actions needed to achieve your goal, you'll be like a motorist driving your car for a long, long trip without first checking how much gas or diesel you have left in your fuel tank. You just won't know what time you'll reach your destination because you'll be very likely to run out of fuel along the way.

A powerful time-management tool, the so-called "Eisenhower Decision Matrix," can greatly help you in figuring the best way to make the schedule for undertaking your action plans. This matrix was popularized in the book *The 7 Habits of Highly Effective People*by Stephen Covey, the popular American educator, author, businessman, and keynote speaker.

The Eisenhower Decision Matrix prompts the decision-maker to clearly distinguish between what's important and what's not important, and between what's urgent and what's not urgent in the action plan.

To make these distinctions easy to grasp, the matrix puts them inside a square divided into four boxes, or quadrants, and specifically labels them as follows:

THE EISENHOWER DECISION MATRIX

Quadrant 1: Urgent but Important;
Quadrant 2: Not Urgent but Important;
Quadrant 3: Urgent but Not Important; and
Quadrant 4: Not Urgent and Not Important.

Below, in diminishing importance, is how the each of the four quadrants in the Eisenhower Decision Matrix classifies and describes the actions or tasks that we need to spend our time on to effectively implement an action plan:

Quadrant 1 (Q1): Urgent but Important Tasks. They require our immediate attention and typically consist of crises, problems, or deadlines.

Typical Q1 workaday examples are the following:

1. Certain e-mails about a possible job offer, new business opportunity, etc.,that requires immediate action
2. A term-paper deadline
3. A mortgage deadline
4. A family member getting into an emergency situation
5. Your car engine conks out unexpectedly
6. Household chores that need be done promptly
7. Getting and answering a call from the school principal about your child's unacceptable behavior.

Quadrant 2 (Q2): Not Urgent but Important Tasks. Activities that don't have a pressing deadline, but nonetheless help you achieve your important personal, school, and work goals. These are typically centered on strengthening relationships, planning for the future, and improving yourself.

Typical workaday Q2 examples are the following:

1. Weekly, monthly, or long-term planning
2. Exercising
3. Family time
4. Reading life-enriching books
5. Journaling
6. Taking a class to improve a skill
7. Studying
8. Meditating
9. Community Service

10. Car and home maintenance
11. Outing with family
12. Creating a budget and a savings plan

We should seek to spend most of our time on Q2 activities, as they are the ones that can provide us lasting happiness, fulfillment, and success. You need to firmly tell yourself: "I'm going to make time for these things come hell or high water."

Quadrant 3 (Q3): Urgent but Not Important Tasks. Activities that require our attention now but not really that important to achieving our goals or fulfilling our mission. Most Q3 tasks are interruptions from other people and often involve helping them meet their own goals and fulfill their own priorities.

Typical Q3 workaday examples are the following:

1. Phone calls
2. Text messages
3. Most e-mails (some e-mails could be urgent and important)
4. Coworker who comes by your desk during your prime working time to ask for a favor
5. Request from a former employee to write a letter of recommendation on his behalf (it's probably important to him, but let's face it, it's probably not that important to you)
6. Your Mom drops in unannounced and wants your help with a chore

Many people spend most of their time on Q3 tasks, all the while thinking that they're working on Q1's. Because Q3 tasks *do* help others out, they definitely feel important. Since they're also usually tangible tasks, their completion can give a sense of satisfaction that comes from doing and later checking that task off your list.

But while getting Q3 tasks may be important to others, they're not that important to you. That doesn't make them necessarily bad, of course, but you need to balance them with your Q2 activities. Otherwise, you could end up feeling like you're getting a lot done from day-to-day, but eventually realize that as a result, you aren't making any progress in your own long-term goals. That could become a recipe for personal frustration and resentment towards other people who bug you much too often to do Q3 tasks for them or on their behalf.

Those who give more time working on Q3 tasks often suffer from what's called the "Nice Guy Syndrome." They have a strong tendency to please others at the expense of their own personal interest or happiness. If that's what you think you are, a Q3 person, the solution is simple: Be more assertive and start to firmly (but politely) say no to most requests.

Quadrant 4 (Q4): Not Urgent and Not Important Tasks. Activities that aren't urgent and aren't really important. They're primarily distractions.

Typical workaday examples are the following:

1. Watching TV
2. Mindlessly surfing the web
3. Playing video games
4. Scrolling through Facebook, Twitter, and Instagram excessively
5. Habitual gambling
6. Shopping sprees

Overall, the Eisenhower Decision Matrix—which by the way is also known as the "Urgent-Important Matrix," can be very useful in helping us decide which tasks in our lives must be given priority. That will make us more effective in accomplishing our goals.

But one question before we leave the subject of goal setting: "Should your personal written goals just be confined in your discreet notebook?"

No, they shouldn't be; on the contrary, your goals have to be visible to you at all times; that way you won't lose focus or forget about them. Keep your written goals in your wallet, make them a background of your laptop, and stick them on your bedroom mirror or on your refrigerator door. When your attention is fixated on achieving your goals, you can create a lasting image of success in your brain.

CHAPTER 5

Establish Deeper Personal Relationships In Your Own Life

"Personal relationships are the fertile soil from which all advancement, all success, all achievement in real life grows."—Benjamin Jeremy Stein, American writer, lawyer, actor, comedian, and commentator (Born 1944)

Are you connecting with the people you love and value in your life? If you do, your life is truly in the right direction. It is just right to have a deep connection with your family, your friends, and other people who are directly or indirectly a part of your life. On top of this, of course, you likewise must nurture a deep connection to God because without Him, we just won't be around in the first place to treasure and enjoy the beauty of life.

When we establish and cultivate a deep and abiding human and social connection with the people around us, it shows and demonstrates our unconditional love and caring for them. We are confident that those who receive our unconditional love and trust would reciprocate and give us comfort in our own times of adversity and sorrow.

On May 8, 2019, when I was writing this chapter, I was still going through a period of mourning over the death of my brother-in-law Floyd O'hara two days before in Chicago, Illinois. A heavy equipment operator and mechanic, Noy Floyd was also an avid electronic enthusiast who could restore a 1960s phonograph by sourcing the replacement parts from outdated electronic devices. He had been diagnosed with Stage 4 cancer of the bladder and passed away just two weeks later.

Noy Floyd became a widower when my sister Teofista died of cervical cancer in 2016; she had a Ph.D in Physics and was the school principal of the Suba Masulog High School and Mactan Air Base High School, both in Lapu-Lapu City. Mourning for Noy Floyd in Chicago were his four grown-up children with Teofista, namely my nieces Aleth, Floydeth, and Patrice and my nephew Charles, as well as members of their respective families.

At the time of Noy Floyd's wake in Chicago I happened to be in Texas, but owing to totally unexpected and unavoidable personal circumstances, it literally became impossible for me to fly to Chicago to pay my respects to his bereaved family. I thus strongly felt that I should at least post on Facebook my condolences to the children.

Tears welled from my eyes when I wrote and posted this message for them: "Losing a loved one is hard, but knowing you have people to walk you through the difficult journey may lighten the grief. You will always have me at your back." It was my own little way of commiserating with them and assuring them of my love and deep affection in their time of sorrow.

Inside our heart lies an abundance of goodness and kindness that we can use to express, strengthen, or revive our familial and social bonds during times of difficulty or adversity in our life's journeys. Thus, when you've cultivated enduring and deep social and familial relationships, you won't hesitate to seek help from your friends, from colleague and mentors, and from family members and other relatives when you encounter adversities and misfortunes in your own life. When you yourself ask them for help, they will also find it so difficult in their hearts to refuse you.

Make every effort then to make your immediate family members understand and sympathize with you in the pursuit of your goals. You'd surely find it too difficult to succeed in any major undertaking if you don't get their encouragement and support.

If a serious misunderstanding has developed between you and your parents, in particular, be humble and try your best to reconnect with them. After all, you owe your existence to them in this planet. Try your best as well to reconcile and make amends with any family member or close friend with whom you have had a rift or a falling out.

Sometime ago I chanced upon a Facebook post addressed to me

from a long-time friend of mine. It had this message: "I'm so glad we can tell each other the good, the bad, and the ugly."

The message was from Frankie, my best friend when we were still in both elementary and high school in Cebu. When he posted that message both of us were already living and working in two different places outside our native Philippines, but we have continued to regularly get in touch with each other through social media, doing so even today.

Frankie and I always share our happiness and struggles and even our failures. Each of us recognizes that we are far from perfect. We both take delight in each other's achievements, but we never hesitate to share with each other our life's challenges, disappointments, and outright failures.

True friends will always try to understand your problems and dilemmas and will go out of their way just to give you a helping hand when you're in need. And one of the great blessings of having genuine friends is that you can allow yourself to be foolish or to fool around with them without being judgmental about your mutual foolishness.

The great social circle of life was compared to a tree by Tyler Perry, an American actor, writer, and director. In his plays and films, he had an alter ago—a tough elderly woman named Madea—who would regale audiences with this tree analogy:

"I have this tree analogy when I think of people in my life, be it friends, family, acquaintances, employees, co-workers, whomever... They are all placed inside what I call my tree test. It goes like this:

"LEAF PEOPLE: Some people come into your life and they are like leaves on a tree. They are only there for a season. You can't depend on them or count on them because they are weak and only there to give you shade. Like leaves, they are there to take what they need and as soon as it gets cold or a wind blows in your life they are gone. You can't be angry at them, it's just who they are.

"BRANCH PEOPLE: There are some people who come into your life and they are like branches on a tree. They are stronger than leaves, but you have to be careful with them. They will stick around through most seasons, but if you go through a storm or two in your life it's possible that you could lose them. Most times they break away when it's tough. Although they are stronger than leaves, you have to test them out before you run out there and put all your weight on them. In most cases they can't handle too much weight. But again, you can't be mad with them, it's just who they are.

"ROOT PEOPLE: If you can find some people in your life who are like the roots of a tree then you have found something special. Like the roots of a tree, they are hard to find because they are not trying to be seen. Their only job is to hold you up and help you live a strong and healthy life. If you thrive, they are happy. They stay low key and don't let the world know that they are there. And if you go through an awful storm they will hold you up. Their job is to hold you up, come what may, and to nourish you, feed you and water you.

"Just as a tree has many limbs and many leaves, there are few roots. Look at your own life. How many leaves, branches and roots do you have? What are you in other people's lives?"

CHAPTER 6

Developing Your Skills, Abilities to the Fullest

"One can choose to go back toward safety or forward toward growth. Growth must be chosen again and again; fear must be overcome again and again."
—Abraham Harold Maslow, American psychologist best known for creating Maslow's hierarchy of needs (1908-1970)

The year 2004 was a major if not the most decisive point in my professional career. I'm saying this not to take the opportunity to trot out my CV in this book but simply to put in context what I feel need to be said about the crucial importance of an honest, dispassionate self-appraisal of our own skills and capabilities to compete in the job market.

By 2004, at the age of 46, I had already notched 23 years of work experience after earning in 1981 my B.S. in Commerce, major in management, from the University of San Jose Recoletos in Cebu City, then earning a Master's in Management - Business Management (MM-BM) as a university scholar from the University of the Philippines 11 years later.

I initially worked in the Philippines, first for a one-year stint as college instructor in marketing and management at the PAFTA College in Lapu-Lapu City, then moving to Manila in late 1984 where I worked for six months as human resource manager of MIC's Construction, a company building military ammunition depots nationwide, which later assigned me to construction project in Tacloban City.

After that, in 1985, I signed up for a Middle East overseas job contract as site field laborer for a trading and contracting company in Riyadh, Saudi Arabia, which assigned me to its Wadi Al-Dawasir unit, about 380 miles away from Riyadh City.

When I finished that contract in 1987, I moved to a Jeddah-based construction company owned by a Saudi Prince for two years of contract work until 1990 as executive secretary. That contract over, I flew back to the Philippines, took up my master's degree until 1992 at the University of the Philippines. This was while I worked as marketing manager and systems consultant for a Cebu City computer-telecom services firm.

In 1993, the lure of overseas contract work once again took me back to the Middle East. I was recruited as executive secretary and administrative project head for an Al-Khobar-based consulting firm that assigned me to service Saudi Aramco, the world's biggest oil producer at that time. The same consulting company subsequently reassigned me to Saudi Aramco itself in Jeddah as executive secretary, reporting directly to the Saudi Aramco Vice President.

When my contract ended seven years later, I flew back to the Philippines in 2000 and founded the Cabahug Management Consultancy—my own company—based in Valenzuela City in Metro Manila. That consulting firm of mine ran for only a little over a year, however, for in 2001 I was offered a new work contract by another consultancy firm servicing Saudi Aramco, this time as a senior project support supervisor based in Al-Khobar, Saudi Arabia.

I must admit that I was overjoyed by that sudden and unexpected bigger assignment. It made me overconfident, believing that my qualifications and work exposure in human resources administration at that time already qualified me to aspire for bigger managerial responsibilities.

So, after just several years as executive secretary in the Saudi Aramco affiliate, I decided to no longer renew my contract with the company. I started applying for managerial positions in other big Middle East companies, confident that I'd get one before my contract for my current job lapsed.

In one of the big Middle East companies that I applied for a managerial position, I handily passed the written examination and aced the preliminary interview. This made me even more confident and jubilant. There was no more doubt in my mind that I'd get that managerial job, finally making the big time among Filipinos in the Middle East doing my work specialty.

But my jubilation vanished when the company formally evaluated my work experience for the managerial position. The formal evaluation stated unequivocally that I didn't have sufficient skills and experience for what I applied for. I was unfit for the job. The long and short of it was that I failed to meet the grade.

So there I was in 2004 in the hot, sweltering port city of Jeddah, jobless after deliberately not renewing my job contract with the Saudi Aramco affiliate and allowing that contract to expire before I got another job in its place! This left me with no other recourse but to fly back to the Philippines totally disillusioned.

But as the cliché says, when life hands you lemons the best thing to do is to make lemonade out of them.

When I got back to Cebu City, I first took an interim teaching job in a computer college as an instructor in office management, MIS-professional ethics, and human behavior in organizations, among several other subjects. Then after only four months, I quit the job and—you'd probably think I'm joking to make light of my disappointment and frustration—I put up a single-proprietorship firm that produced lemonade products and did catering jobs.

With me as general manager, the business sold and distributed the "Honey Lemonade" brand of juice drink to direct consumers and retailers in Luzon and the Visayas, at the same time catering lunch for employees daily in over 20 banks in Cebu City, Lapu-Lapu City, and Mandaue City. The business ran successfully and profitably enough for almost two years until I finally decided to close it down in 2007 for a reason that I'll be discussing later in this book.

I've given lots of details about how my own professional career evolved—with many of its twists and turns, so speak—to emphasize this very important point: If you want to achieve your goal, you need to develop your personal skills, abilities, and character the best you can. They will be the foundation of how strong you'll be in pursuing your life's goals; altogether, they can be a powerful motive force that can make you achieve big things and make you something larger than yourself.

Have you heard the saying that while it's undeniably true that formal education can give us a living, it's our own personal life experience that can give us a fortune? You better believe it! In my case it's true and I swear by it.

Phenomenally successful entrepreneurs and technology-savvy individuals like Facebook co-founder Mark Zuckerberg as well as Microsoft Corporation co-founder Bill Gates both weren't able to finish college, but they both accomplished their respective great visions in life because they used the biggest learning center in the universe—their life experience—to improve their skills and capabilities.

So, no matter if you've already attained many of your life's goals, never stop learning, for your learning doesn't have to end after school; it should be a lifetime commitment. The environment around us is our largest library for learning, and it's where we should become warriors for life.

Once learning stops, life becomes dull and uninteresting and uneventful. If your own life has become like that, you'd lose the appetite to do the action work needed to fast-forward your dreams and aspirations.

Your personal development won't only involve feeding your mind with knowledge, however. Even more important, you need to take good care of your health. Cultivating your mind must always come hand-in-hand with taking good care of your body.

Take a close look at the figure below. It's called "The Triangular Dimension for Self-development" and it shows us these three aspects of our life: our Intelligence Quotient (IQ), our Emotional Quotient (EQ), our Adversity Quotient (AQ), and our Spiritual Quotient (SQ).

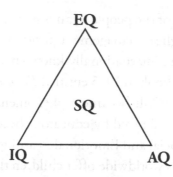

THE TRIANGULAR DIMENSION FOR SELF-DEVELOPMENT

1. Intelligence Quotient (IQ)—This is your ability to use our mental or cognitive capacity and to reason out. There are many ways to improve it. You can continue to hone the skills that you already have or to learn to do new things that you've never done before—things like solving crossword puzzles, analyzing complicated subjects, or solving mathematical problems.

To boost your energy level and sharpen your mental faculties, you need to engage in regular exercise, like playing the sports you love or just doing simple brisk walking. Research published in the Proceedings of the National Academy of Sciences show that people who exercise tend to have higher IQ scores than those who don't. This is because exercise stimulates brain cell growth through a process called neurogenesis; exercise floods the brain with pleasurable neurotransmitters such as dopamine, which promote our well-being.

Also, having the good balanced diet can give you more than just a healthy body; it also helps sharpen your memory, improve your test scores, and give you a pleasant mood.

2. Emotional Quotient (EQ)—This is our ability to recognize and cope with our own feelings in times of adversity and frustration. Emotional intelligence is one of the most important factors for a person's success in life; it accounts for anywhere from 24% to 69% of performance success in the workplace. Indeed, human resource managers are very familiar with EQ because it's a good tool for identifying and measuring the "soft people skills" of the people in an organization, from the lowest ranked staff to the highest management positions.

Daniel Goleman, an internationally-known psychologist and science journalist, published a book in 1955 entitled *Emotional Intelligence: Why it mattered more than IQ*. It became a phenomenal best-seller and his EQ concept has been embraced by educators, becoming the basis for a program known as "Social and Emotional Learning," or SEL. Now, tens of thousands of schools worldwide offer children the SEL program, and many companies today use the EQ concept to increase their chances of successfully getting a good selection of staff hires.

3. Adversity Quotient (AQ)—This is our ability to survive and overcome extreme obstacles in life. It's a combination of one's higher emotional quotient and one's survival capability. A very simple example of an Adversity Quotient is this: When you're thrown into shark-infested waters, your higher Adversity Quotient will fuel your ability to reach the surface immediately before the sharks bite and tear you into pieces.

A high AQ will enable you to do everything in your power to survive; it will make you act fast, think fast, and do things at the right moment. In the workplace, the Adversity Quotient is used to determine if staff and managers are fully energized and resilient in overcoming the perils of their work. If you have weak AQ, you'd find it difficult keep up your efficiency and the effectiveness level of your abilities and skills.

4. Spiritual Quotient (SQ)—This is the larger-than-life inside and center of the Triangular Dimension for Self-Development. Our SQ is the level of our self-awareness that we are a creation of God. It is our spontaneous acknowledgment that it would be very difficult for us to achieve our goals if we just rely on our knowledge, skills and abilities in tackling the turmoil of everyday life. It is the source of our self-assurance that if we take good care of the spiritual aspects of our lives, we can expect to reap joy and happiness.

Your talents and skills are not something inborn; they have to be developed and nurtured through time both by hard work and by working smarter. A commonly observed rule for people to be able to work smarter is to follow the 80/20 rule. This rule means that to fast track your goal, you must prioritize two out of every ten tasks of yours as the most urgent and important tasks to be dealt with right away.

And to succeed in pursuing your goals, you must never stop believing that you can take advantage of any opportunity in your life by growing and developing you skills and abilities to the fullest. This is a powerful mantra that truly works and successful people most everywhere in the world believe it and say it to inspire and empower themselves at all times.

CHAPTER 7

Fully Identify Your Own Inner Strengths

"You really have to look inside yourself and find your own inner strength, and say, 'I'm proud of what I am and who I am, and I'm just going to be myself.'"
—*Mariah Carey, American singer-songwriter, record producer, actress, entrepreneur, and philanthropist*
(Born 1970)

When you want to sell your house or perhaps your car that you want replaced with a newer model, you'll seek the expert opinion of other people to appraise its current market value or resale value. The most reliable people to do the assessment for the house are, of course, reputable real estate agents in your locality and the local city assessor; and for your car, it would be local car dealers of known probity and fair dealing. You need their expertise and wisdom to figure out the best resale price for your two valuable possessions that you're selling.

For an assessment of your life and career, however, of much greater value is the limitless self-abundance that resides inside you. You need somebody other than yourself—someone who knows you very well—to evaluate your self-value or self-worth. It won't do for you to set all alone the price tag for yourself, for if you do that, you'd likely end up undervaluing your true worth. This is because like most everybody else in that situation, you'd tend to concentrate on and magnify your weaknesses rather than focus on your strengths.

Take a look at what usually happens in your workplace. When your boss decides to assign you to do a challenging and unfamiliar task, your own mind automatically begins to do a self-talk questioning your capability for accomplishing it. That negative self-talk—thoughts like "What if I fail?", "There's not enough time for me to finish that assignment!", and "I don't have the competence and skills to do it!"—pummels your brain and invariably erodes your self-confidence. You'll likely accept the assignment halfheartedly, grudgingly, to the consternation and disappointment of your boss.

With today's dizzying stream of technological advances, many people do get overwhelmed and find it difficult to cope with them, often leading to an acute sense of dissatisfaction with themselves. I'll admit that I'm one of them. This poor, low self-perception can often cause us great mental and emotional pain that blocks our way to getting our goals and day-to-day tasks done.

The fact is that many of us choose to hang our positive self-image in the valley down a mountain rather than at the top of that mountain. Still, we can always change that picture by an act of will. We can motivate ourselves to fast-track our journey to accomplishment and success by imagining ourselves at the top of the mountain instead, looking down at the valuable prize that we're after. The sight of it from that high vantage point can make that prize look so tempting, so irresistible, and so energizing that it becomes an absolute must for us to get hold of it in the shortest time possible!

Speaking of personal weaknesses, I used to have one weakness too strong that I think it's worth sharing my experience with it in this book: I'm too trusting of people, even those whom I've just met, as a result of which I've often been stabbed at the back to my deep regret.

Right after graduating from college in 1981, I started a small handicraft business in Mandaue City that made necklaces, bracelets, and earrings from coconut shells. To help me run it, I hired a new friend of mine—let's just call him Rey here to protect his identity and privacy—who I had been told by my other friends was a good and trustworthy worker.

He was excellent in producing pastel colors, in sourcing raw materials, in establishing good relations with exporters, and in ensuring the quality of finished products. His performance in helping me get the business on-stream impressed me, and he gave me no reason to doubt that he could be a good long-term partner who could make my handicraft business grow, prosper, and become profitable

However, it proved very difficult for me to oversee and monitor the progress of that handicraft business of mine while I was in Jeddah, Saudi Arabia over 5,600 miles away, working as executive secretary for a group of companies owned by the Prince of Saudi Arabia.

As the island of Cebu didn't have Internet connectivity yet at that time, my only way to communicate with Rey was through snail-mail, parcel post, and calls either by landline long-distance phone or analog cellular phone. My conference calls with our customers in the Philippines thus had to very short and sketchy, for they were costing me a fortune in interconnection fees.

So I guess there's no need for me to say where this story of mine is leading to. One night, in my accommodation flat in Jeddah (it was of course night in Cebu in the Philippines), I got a long and painful cellular phone call from a family member. In a doleful tone she told me that the profit margins of the handicraft business had gone seriously down and she recited to me a litany of reasons for that bad state of affairs.

I already had strong suspicions about why the business was experiencing those problems but I held back, telling Rey just to do his best to put the business on better financial footing. My great mistake at that point, however, was that I continued trusting him, so great was my faith that he was a great friend of mine and couldn't purposely do me wrong.

A few days later, after making several frantic calls to my relatives in Cebu, I found out that the real reason why that handicraft business of mine was failing so miserably. Rey, as the overall in-charge, seriously mismanaged it.

Our main client, the exporter of the women's accessories to the United States and Europe, had terminated our suppliership agreement for cause and abandoned us. They got terribly upset by our company's performance, very angry over the poor quality of our products, and furious over the serious delays in their deliveries to them.

In language pure and simple, that handicraft venture of mine had too soon turned into a business fiasco. It had become an unreliable supplier and an unprofitable enterprise. So, after running it for only eight months more, I asked a family member to close it down for good. I said goodbye to its seven employees and terminated Rey.

Looking back, I realized with great regret that I had trusted him too much just out of friendship and not much else.

As a result of that experience, I became deathly afraid of taking risks in anything in my subsequent pursuits as an entrepreneur. The mere thought of failure owing to a bad decision would send shivers up my spine. I'd since become much more careful in choosing my friends. With regard to financial matters, I now take only very well-calculated risks and only in something that I'm truly passionate about.

Having suffered from poorly calculated risk-taking, I've become a firm believer in systematic approaches to solving problems and in continual innovation in every enterprise that I'd put a stake in. For as one success guru was once quoted saying, "If you will not innovate you will evaporate!" Truly, you won't grow if you keep on doing the same unchallenging things and keep on living in the same safe, risk-free, and comfortable spot.

If you already know your strengths, however, you need to likewise identify your weaknesses and make every effort to find solutions for overcoming them. Always remember that all of us in this world have weaknesses, and that the best way to deal with those weaknesses is to first identify them and then to use as much of the resources in our command to conquer them.

In our own personal lives, of course, there will be bad days when we could lose the motivation to accomplish the tasks we need to reach our goals. What can we do to regain that strong motivation, that fire in our inner being, that inner passion that makes us accomplish those tasks and even more challenging things in our life?

I think that what can light that fire again is a much clearer and deeper understanding of our very own life purpose.

This reminds me of an exciting story told about David Livingstone, the 18th century Scottish explorer, physician, and pioneer Christian missionary whose exploration of the Nile River and the central African watershed became the high point of the period of European geographical discovery and colonial penetration of Africa.

A search for the missing Livingstone in Africa—that was when the outside world completely lost contact with him for six years—became the subject of the famous book *How I Found Livingstone*, a first-hand account written by the Welsh-American journalist and explorer Sir Henry Morton Stanley.

In 1866, Stanley found Livingstone in the depths of the Congo after searching for him for six years. Then, back in England after the publication of Stanley's book, Livingstone was asked the following question by a group of explorers: "Have you found a good road to where you are? If so, we want to know how to send other men to join you."

Livingstone's curt reply: "If you have men who will come only if they know there is a good road, I don't want them. I want men who will come even if there is no road at all."

Of course, what Livingstone clearly implied in that advice is this: that people are not obligated to follow the well-beaten, well-travelled road that had been taken by others. They need to look for and travel their own roads that will lead them to the goals of their own respective life journeys. If that road taken proves to be a wrong one, one has to graciously admit the mistake and then look for the correct road to the correct destination.

When acknowledging their having made a mistake, people often say this classic excuse: "To err is human." I think we can all agree that saying that line just isn't enough. We need to make amends for our mistakes—to sincerely apologize for them—so we can carry on with our lives with dignity and without guilt.

Always keep in mind this often-quoted adage: "It is easier to move from failure to success than from excuses to success." You'd demonstrate that you are a better person the moment you own up your weakness.

I think it would be pertinent at this point to ask ourselves: "What kind of strength or strengths should we develop to become a better person?"

One obvious answer is physical strength, but I'm sure that you'll agree that physical strength just isn't enough. On top of physical strength, what we need is the kind of strength that transcends the physical. We need to possess that strong inner strength to transform our life into what we want our life to become—a life infused with the timeless virtues of character, integrity, honesty, kindness, sociability, empathy, and compassion.

A business model that I used to teach in the subject of Business Policy in the Kingdom of Bahrain is the so-called "SWOT Analysis." It's a scanning device that compares the inner strengths and weaknesses of people in relation to their internal and external environments.

The first two variables in the "SWOT analysis" model are Strengths (S) and Weaknesses (W), which are your internal attributes or qualities over which you have a direct control. The next two variables are Opportunity (O) and Threats (T), which are your attributes or external qualities over which you have no control, but are in a good position to choose how best to respond to them.

The "strength" that you know is deep inside you is your best quality or attribute; it can grow exponentially if you harness and develop it well. On the other hand, your "weaknesses" are your internal attributes that are holding back your progress; you have to resolve these negative qualities of yours as early as possible to prevent you from getting stagnant.

The Opportunity (O) is an external factor that you should take advantage of by taking the appropriate action. When you've prepared yourself for an opportunity, would you be ready to seize it the very moment it presents itself? Preparation and action are the two buzz words for successfully seizing an opportunity.

Lastly, the "Threat" (T) is an external factor that will pin you down if you never act on it decisively and right on time.

You can undertake a SWOT Analysis for your own life once you've made a firm commitment to change your attitude and mindset and to do things differently afterwards for your own advantage. But you need not wait. You can privately do it now if you want or need to. It's a powerful way to acknowledge your weaknesses, that you aren't perfect. Truly, it's a virtuous act to seek to discover your own weak points and make an effort to improve them.

Several years ago in the United States, as some family members and

I sat down for dinner in a downtown Chinese restaurant in Kerville, Texas, the head waiter gave each of us a fortune cookie.

Mine yielded a small strip of paper with this Chinese proverb in English: *"Behavior is a mirror in which everyone shows his own image."*

How wise and apropos that adage was—and still is! All of our deeds in life will indeed always be reflective of our own behavior and of how we've developed ourselves to be better persons. It's very important, particularly when we're feeling so down and weary, to look ourselves up in the mirror and say out loud that we are strong, that we are resolute, that we are gifted with our strong inner strength to overcome life's adversity.

We should stop needlessly spending valuable time thinking of what can't be done rather than focusing on what can be done. We need to give ourselves more time to cultivate our self-confidence and our self-esteem.

In front of the mirror we can softly but purposively chant superlative positive exhortations to ourselves like, say, "I am a kind-hearted individual," "I can make the lives of other people happy," "I am making a big difference in this world," or "I will achieve my goals because I always act on them daily."

When you make it a habit to tell yourself those powerful mantras, you're much more likely to achieve your vision in life because you will actually be rewiring your brain to change your attitude so you can do things the best way you can.

CHAPTER 8

Distinguish a Career From a Calling

"Choose a job you love and you will never have to work a day in your life."—***Confucius,*** ***Chinese philosopher and politician*** ***(551-479 BC)***

How do you differentiate a career from a calling?

There's obviously a big difference between the two. A career is planned and intended, while a calling is something you pursue because you feel strongly passionate about it.

Very simply said, you decide your career, but you discover your calling.

Imagine how problematic it can become when the parents themselves decide the future of their children!

Let's say one of the kids wants to become a doctor and the Mom or Dad tells him to take up the course in Medicine. The boy probably has no clue yet as to what he wants to be in life, but becoming a doctor just rang a bell inside his brain. But when the time comes for that boy to get more aware of his own talents, abilities, and needs, that's when the real-world problem of getting a medical degree starts to stare him in the face.

I know someone who decided to take up Nursing because her elder sister happened to be a successful nurse, but she encountered great difficulty and hardship from the very first year of her studies. No matter how hard she studied her subjects, she'd get failing grades in not just a few of them.

The culprit? Her interest turned out to be not in health care but in management. So she wasted an entire year in a course that really wasn't for her, aptitude-wise! Ultimately, however, she was very thankful that her parents agreed with her decision to shift to something much better suited to her and much more to her liking—business management.

When you do or pursue something that you're truly passionate about, your life becomes much more meaningful. Your career or calling becomes your constant companion no matter where you go. It will get you to see better of yourself and motivate you to achieve your potential to the fullest.

Indeed, pursuing a career of your own choice becomes an abiding source of extrinsic motivation for you; you'll feel truly happy with the external rewards that you'll reap from it, such as salary, promotion, a good reputation or perhaps even fame.

In contrast, a calling provides you with an intrinsic motivation, one in which your heart's desire drives your best inner nature to help other people and society in general to achieve their goals, realize their true worth, and promote their welfare and well-being.

Do you remember doing a very difficult task but despite the constant adversity you encountered, you weren't discouraged but became even more relentless in doing it? If so, you're a very passionate individual. No amount of roadblocks and obstacles can stop you from pursuing the things you love to do.

I still recall that in the MBA class that I was teaching in 2018, a student asked me this rather testy question: "Sir, what type of business do you think is feasible today and that's really worth my money to invest in?"

My quick and categorical answer was this: "I don't know."

The whole class stared at me in disbelief!

At this point I asked one of them to stand up and I posed this question pointblank: "What's your passion in life and what are the things that you love to do?"

The guy excitedly said in so many words that since his primary school days and all through high school and even at that very day, he had always wanted to draw or paint on any surface—paper, walls, blackboards or whiteboards, anything at all!—especially if the drawing or painting is about nature and the world around him.

"Aha!" I told him, to the delight of the whole class. "Now you have come up with the most feasible business you'd like to have considering the things that you really love to do—paint landscapes and portraits and your own art gallery to sell them!"

My point here is that if you have an entrepreneurial bent and engage in a business that's close to your heart, you've already met the very first success criterion for doing a business, one much more crucial than the money you'd be making from it.

But why?

It's simply because when you're doing the things you love to do, it ignites the fire in your belly, so to speak. That fire will be so strong that even if you fail in solving a problem in the first or even in many more attempts, you just won't give up.

You'll continue to seek out solutions in or outside the box, even turning that box upside down to solve that problem. You won't ever do this if your business is one that you don't love strongly enough; you'll likely quit even just at the first sign that you'll fail.

Let me tell you the story about life as a four-letter word. You've probably heard that story before, but I think it's worth listening to again.

It goes like this:

Most of us see **LIFE** as a four-letter word but it's actually an acronym for the four stages of living in this world.

"L" represents the stage of "LEARNING." It's when you lay down the foundation upon which the whole reach of your life would be based—your thoughts, your attitudes, your emotions, and your associations with others.

"I" represents the stage of "INTIMACY." It's that stage when you find out things for yourself and when you develop your habits that will make you what you'll become.

"F" represents the stage of "FAME." It's that stage when you attain your greatest successes and experience your worst failures.

And last, "E" represents the stage of "ETERNITY." It's that stage when you cultivate those strong forces and vibrations that will create a presence that will continue to grow even beyond your lifetime."

In sum, LIFE is a four-stage thing that's always full of richness.

To live it joyfully you've got to take advantage of all the wealth and blessings it offers you.

Today, I'm running a small management consultancy in Cebu and Manila that every now and then conducts pro bono seminars to companies. Money remains important to me, of course, but it's no longer my primary consideration for doing the things that I love to do.

What really matters most to me now is the feel of pure joy and excitement in fulfilling my innermost drive, which is to share with others whatever little bounty of knowledge I've acquired in my life by far. And as I pursue this habit, which is what I would now call my calling, I find that I'm also improving my skills as well as developing the attributes that I find within me.

As an upshot of this passion of mine, I've been able to establish a wider network of friends, friends who became my clients, clients who in turn might recommend me to other potential clients.

By continually doing this, not only do I help others; I also improve my craft and get financial rewards from doing so. This way, too, I'm able to retool my skills and improve my own fund of knowledge while doing the very things that matters most in my life.

Another important thought that I'd like to share at this point: *No one gets rich working for another!* In the Philippines, there's a very popular belief that goes like this: "Filipino parents send their children to school so they can find a job, but Chinese parents send their children to school so they can put up a business after graduation." I guess—and correct me if I'm wrong—this is precisely the reason why the richest person in the Philippines is of Chinese origin!

There's actually no problem with working for others, but the bigger question is: "Would you rather spend all your life working for others when you can engage in something on your own, something you're most passionate about, to attain success in life?"

Think about this before answering that question: Research has established that we spend one-third of our lives working until we retire—meaning an average of 90,000 hours over our whole lifetime of work.

You'd probably find it incredible that in 1985, during my first stint in the Kingdom of Saudi Arabia as an OFW (that stands for "overseas Filipino worker" or "overseas foreign worker," of course—take your pick), I received a meager monthly salary of only US$210. That salary was comparable to that of a construction worker in Saudi at that time!

I needed to augment my income to survive, of course, so I had to find some additional sources to keep myself afloat, so to speak. I sold cassette tapes to our co-workers of different nationalities inside our work camp. I gave free *"hilot"* or massage to fellow Filipinos who'd get injured while playing basketball or tennis.

One exception I imposed on myself though: not to accept money in payment for that very personal service. This is because I've always thought that in a foreign land, we should be all compassionate to others by sharing our talents and abilities gratis *et amore* or without asking payment for it.

For that act of kindness, though, I'd be paid in kind instead, like meals, snacks, or new tennis balls. This allowed me to earn some money for my personal expenses, on top of my meager income as a construction worker in the Middle East desert.

That experience in a place over 25,000 miles from my homeland gave me this priceless lesson: No matter how awful your situation might be, you can always rise above the situation.

CHAPTER 9

20 Notable Filipino Achievers In Their Careers or Callings

"Dreams are free, so why limit what you are aspiring for? But dreaming is not enough. One needs to put in enough energy and input."—Tony Tan-Caktiong, founder of the fast-food chain Jollibee Corporation (Born 1953)

In the preceding chapter we took up the need to clearly differentiate between a career and a calling. A *career* is planned and intended, while a *calling* is something you pursue because you feel strongly passionate about it.

In short, you decide your career, but you discover your calling.

I said that pursuing something that you're truly passionate about will get you to see better of yourself and motivate you to achieve your potential to the fullest. Whether you decide to pursue a career or practice a calling, you'll feel truly happy with the external rewards that you'll reap from it, such as a good salary or income, getting promoted, or acquiring a good reputation or perhaps even fame in your chosen field.

However, we must keep in mind that getting to pursue the career or calling that's closest to our heart sometimes can get tough and complicated—even emotionally wrenching. One common reason for this is succumbing to the wishes of our parents.

Among us Filipinos, in particular, we are traditionally very obedient to our Moms and Dads when it comes to choosing what course or degree to pursue in college. In a typical Filipino family, in fact, it's considered terribly disrespectful and even taboo for kids to disobey parents and take a course not to their liking.

In 2018, for instance, I was shocked by what I was told by a 27-year-old businesswoman student of mine in the ETEEAP course (Expanded Tertiary Education Equivalency Accreditation Program) that I was teaching at the University of San Jose Recoletos in Cebu City. I'll just identify her as Steff B. to protect her identity and privacy.

Steff talked to me about her 10-year-old daughter Debbie, confiding to me in a voice of such terrifying finality that she had already implanted in her daughter's mind that she should become a doctor when she grows up.

Aghast but speaking in the most composed voice that I could muster, I asked Steff: "And how did Debbie react to that?"

"Oh, Debbie is a very good girl and she dutifully agreed to be a doctor," Steff said. "She has become very excited by that prospect. Except that I'm now having a big problem with her. Twice already, she'd get so upset whenever she makes just one or two mistakes in her science exams. She'd get so terrified by those mistakes in her science-related subjects, bursting into tears at the thought that they just might cause her not to become a doctor someday."

This is the great danger when parents tyrannically design the future of their kids and don't give them a chance to decide on their own. As a result of this, they'd oftentimes rebel and might even run away from home and—God forbid!—possibly become a menace to society. Indeed, kids who have arrived on a definite purpose in their life might drop out of school, then pursue on their own their life's calling but hopefully achieve success nevertheless.

To achieve success in life, however, you don't necessarily need a college degree; it's your own calling that will enable you to reach your goals in life.

It won't matter very much whether you're a college degree holder or school drop-out. The most important thing is that despite whatever setback might come, you're able to follow your passion without letup.

Remember that wise admonition? "We are not upset by what happens, but by our interpretation of what happens."

A shining example is Bill Gates, the co-founder of Microsoft that today is the world's Number 1 computer software company. He didn't finish college because he greatly trusted his own instincts, then followed his calling to write the Windows computer program and establish his own software company. In fact, he's undoubtedly the most successful college dropout and wealthiest individual in the world today.

You need to follow your own path so that you'll experience a happy and fruitful life and, through your own initiative and creativity, be able to do something new or something exceptional that can propel your growth to the fullest.

Of course, it's likewise very important to know the roads travelled and the challenges hurdled by highly accomplished real-life people to achieve notable success in their respective careers and callings—the better for all of us to draw inspiration and nuggets of wisdom on how to shape our own lives and follow our own dreams.

With that in mind, I've collected and put together in capsule form the inspiring life stories of 20 Filipinos—10 men and 10 women—who have successfully pursued their respective careers or callings in our time between the 1940s onwards to the present.

To highlight the remarkable diversity of their accomplishments and to eschew gender bias, I departed from the predictable dispassionate manner of listing them that's typically adopted by award-giving bodies and the mass media.

So, according to age in a successive alternate male/female order each time, and not necessarily in the order of accomplishment, wealth, or popularity, here now is my personal list of 20 notable Filipinos that I believe are worthy of being role models in their respective careers or callings:

Socorro Ramos, entrepreneur (bookstores and school supplies)

Henry Sy Sr., businessman (supermarkets and real estate)

John Gokongwei Jr., businessman (supermarkets and food manufacturing)

Julie Gandiongco, businesswoman (bakeshops and bakeshop franchising)

Lucio Tan, businessman (beer and tobacco manufacturing, airlines)

Corazon D. Ong, entrepreneur (meat processing)

Diosdado Banatao, computer technology design (electrical engineer)

Manuel (Manny) Villar Jr., businessman (real estate, malls, convenience stores)

Lea Salonga, international singer and stage actress

Tony Tan Caktiong, businessman (international franchising of hamburger restaurants)

Monique Lhuillier, international entrepreneur (fashion design)

Apl.de.ap (Allan Pineda Lindo), singer and Grammy award-winning performer

Reese Fernandez-Ruiz, social entrepreneur (eco-ethical fashion and home accessories)

Robbie Antonio, international entrepreneur (real estate, modular buildings)

Emmanuel (Manny) Pacquiao, international boxing champion, Philippine senator

Happy Andrada, international fashion designer

Bruno Mars (Peter Gene Hernandez), singer-songwriter, record producer

Mica Tan, businesswoman (international private equity firm)

Charice Pempengco, award-winning singer and international song album bestseller

Natasha Bautista, international model, general manager (GrabTaxi Philippines)

Their nutshell bios are presented in the next pages of this chapter. I invite all of you to look them over now to see how they evolved in their respective careers or callings.

The Careers and Callings of This Book's
20 Outstanding Filipino Achievers

SOCORRO C. RAMOS, 96. The matriarch founder of National Book Store, the largest bookstore chain in the Philippines, Nanay as she is fondly called by her family and business associates has been hailed as the country's champion of entrepreneurship and entrepreneurial thinking. She got into the publishing and retail industry before World War II as a bookstore salesgirl. In 1940, she and her husband Jose rented a small-corner space of a haberdashery at the foot of Escolta Bridge in Santa Cruz, Manila. They set up their first retail bookstore selling GI novels, text books and supplies. During the World War, the store shifted to selling sold candies, soap, and slippers due to stringent book censorship. But the post-war boom in the Philippines from 1946 onwards proved profitable for their venue. Their bookstore and school-supplies business zoomed and the Ramoses were able to put up a nine-story building along Avenida Avenue (now Rizal Avenue). Over the next several decades they put up branch bookstores in major cities all over the country.

HENRY SY SR., 95 (died January 19, 2019). A low-key Filipino business magnate, investor, and philanthropist, Sy was the founder and owner of Shoe Mart (SM) Mall, the largest shopping mall in the Philippines. He became one of the richest men in the world by making SM a world-class commercial center developer, with his various businesses reaching an estimated net worth of US$19 billion. They included 77 SM malls in the Philippines and China, 62 department stores, 56 supermarkets and over 200 grocery stores. SM also owns BDO, the country's second-largest bank. Young Henry and his family used to live in poverty in China and migrated to the Philippines in 1936. They put up a store in Manila but lost it during the World War II bombings. To survive, Henry started to sell used military combat boots and other postwar goods to American soldiers. He then put up the SM network of shopping malls engaged in real-estate development, building high-rise residential condominiums in Metro Manila and in the country's key cities.

JOHN GOKONGWEI JR., 93 (died November 9, 2019). He was the founderof JG Holdings, a major conglomerate engaged in telecommunications, shopping malls, financial services, petrochemicals, power generation, food and beverage, livestock farming, and aviation. His ascendancy in Philippine business is truly a "rich-to-rags-to riches" story. His father was a scion of a wealthy Cebu-based family with ancestral ties to China's Southern Fujian province. Young John attended primary school at the University of San Carlos in Cebu City, graduating valedictorian, and finished high school there. But when John was only 13 years, the Gokongwei family fortune was lost after his father died. To support the family, young John peddled items along the streets of Cebu City's streets from his bicycle and traded various merchandise using a wooden boat, taking his goods by sea to as far as Lucena in Luzon, and then to Manila by truck. In 1977, Gokongwei earned his MBA from De La Salle University in Manila and later attended a 14-week advanced management program at Harvard University. The net worth of his holdings in 2019 was estimated at US$5.3 billion.

JULIE GANDIONCO, 89. The founder of Julie's Bakeshop, Julie Gandionco got into business at age 50 by opening a small "sari-sari" store in Cebu City in 1981. She also accepted sewing jobs from the neighborhood in to augment the family income. Subsequently, she applied as one of the canteen concessionaries in Philcadan, a Mandaue City-based rattan factory. Starting with an initial capital of only P3,000, her canteen business grew to three canteens in the factory, providing the food requirements of more than a thousand workers on a daily basis. With her keen business acumen, Julie saw that there was a huge demand for bread for the daily breakfast and *merienda* of the factory workers, so she decided to embark on another business—the bakery business. Investing her lifetime savings of P19,000, Julie bought second-hand equipment for her own bakeshop. Today, Julie's Bakeshop has become the country's largest bakeshop chain, with 500 franchisee branches all over the Philippines from as far north as Laoag City in the north to Zamboanga City in the south.

LUCIO TAN, 86. A self-made billionaire who once worked as a janitor to put himself through college, Lucio Tan got into business in 1966 by putting up Fortune Tobacco, a self-owned company that in just 15 years became the country's largest cigarette manufacturer. Subsequently, he secured control of the country's flag-carrier Philippine Airlines, becoming its chairman and chief executive officer in 1995. He also acquired Tanduay Holdings, Philippine National Bank, Eton Properties, and the University of the East. Now the Philippines' sixth richest man with an estimated net worth of $3.1 billion, the young Lucio was born in Fujian, China, but his parents moved with him to Cebu in the Philippines when he was a child. Growing up, he first worked as a stevedore who tied cargo with ropes in the hold of ships, then as a janitor at a tobacco factory to pay for his schooling. He had his primary and secondary education at Chiang Kai Shek College in Manila and later earned a B.S. in Chemical Engineering from the Far Eastern University in Manila.

CORAZON D. ONG, 50. The founder of CDO Foodsphere in 1975, Corazon Ong is a professional nutritionist who was hailed as the "Most Outstanding Nutritionist of the Year" nine years before. Hers is a heartwarming story of a mother turned into a successful businesswoman. With her experience as a dietitian, she experimented with a new filling for *siopao*, in addition to the usual *bola-bola* and *asado*. Then she founded CDO Food Products in 1975 at the backyard of the Ongs' house in Valenzuela, Bulacan, with a capital of P60,000 loaned from a local bank. She then used her knowledge to create processed meats affordable enough to compete with popular foreign brands— corned beef, hamburger patties, meat loaf, and hotdogs—initially then purely as a home business. Eventually, she expanded her company to become a household name in quality food products; indeed, for the period 1999-2003, CDO Foodsphere was awarded by the Consumers Union awarded as the country's most outstanding meat processor.

In 1996, for her successful leadership of CDO-Foodsphere, Corazon became the Agora Awardee for the "Most Outstanding Medium-Scale Entrepreneur" given by the Philippine Marketing Association.

DIOSDADO BANATAO, 94. The founder of the three technology firms Mostron, Chips and Technologies, S3 Graphics in the United States, he has been dubbed as the "Bill Gates" of the Philippines. He used to walk barefoot to get his elementary and high school education in a barrio in Cagayan Valley, then finished his electrical engineering degree *cum laude* at the Mapua Institute of Technology in Manila. After college, Banatao turned down several job offers, including one from the electric utility firm Meralco. He joined Philippine Airlines as a trainee pilot and was later pirated by Boeing, where he worked as a design engineer for the company's new commercial airliner and cargo transport aircraft, the Boeing 747. As a working student in the U.S., he completed his Master's in electrical engineering at Stanford University in California. His design capabilities enabled him to develop several milestone products in the computer industry, among them the single-chip controller and chip sets. His Chips and Technologies company was later bought by Intel for a whopping $430 million. His net worth in 2019 was estimated at US$5.3 billion.

MANUEL (MANNY) VILLAR JR., 70. A former Philippine senator whose wife Cynthia is currently also a senator, Manny Villar is the founder of Vista Land & Lifescapes, a real estate conglomerate that started with building residential subdivisions but eventually ventured into condominiums, malls, convenience stores, coffee chains, and a cemetery. As a child, Villar initially attended Isabelo de los Reyes Elementary School, a public school in Tondo, Manila. He assisted his mother in selling shrimp and fish at the Divisoria Public Market to help earn the money to support his siblings and himself to school. He subsequently earned a Masters in business administration from the University of the Philippines, after which he worked as an accountant and financial analyst. Then he launched a highly successful business in real estate, with his companies having built over 200,000 homes thereafter, making him and his family among the wealthiest in the Philippines. Today, he is listed by *Forbes Magazine* as the second richest Filipino with a total net worth of US$6.6 billion.

LEA SALONGA, 49. A Filipina singer, actress, recording artist, and television performer, Lea is best known for her roles in musical theater, having supplied the singing voices of two Walt Disney movie princesses, Jasmine and Mulan. At age 18 she originated the lead role of Kim in the musical *Miss Saigon*, first in the West End and then on Broadway. For her performances in that musical, she won the Olivier and Theatre World Awards and became the first Asian woman to win a Tony Award. Also, Lea is the first Filipino artist to sign with an international record label—with Atlantic Records in 1993—and was the first actress of Asian descent to play the roles of Éponine and Fantine in the musical *Les Misérables* on Broadway. She finished her secondary education in 1988 at the O. B. Montessori Center in Greenhills in San Juan City and attended the University of the Philippines College of Music's extension program aimed at training musically talented children in music and stage movement. Lea made her professional debut in 1978 at age seven in the musical *The King and I* with Repertory Philippines.

TONY TAN CAKTIONG, 67. The founder in 1978 of the highly successful Jollibee Foods restaurant franchise, Tony Tan Caktiong was born to Chinese immigrant parents from Fujian but migrated to the Philippines. He attended high school at Chiang Kai Shek College and graduated from the University of Santo Tomas in 1975 with a degree in chemical engineering. He had initially planned an ice cream parlor when he founded Jollibee, but when the business could not generate enough revenues, he decided to add dishes such as hamburgers, French fries, and fried chicken to its product line. Today, Jollibee has over 2,500 stores in the Philippines and several other outlets in the United States, China, Saudi Arabia, Vietnam, Singapore, and Brunei. Also, Jollibee Foods has since acquired the Philippine food companies Red Ribbon, Chowking, Greenwich, Manong Pepe's and Mang Inasal; it also has invested in the real-estate business through Double Dragon Properties Corporation.

In 2007, Tan was honored as the Philippines' first "Entrepreneur of the Year" by the now-defunct *Entrepreneur Magazine*. As of May 2020, Tan's net worth was estimated at US$1.9 billion.

MONIQUE LHUILLIER, 48. A Filipino fashion designer and creative director known for her own bridal, ready-to-wear and lifestyle brand of dresses, Monique Lhuillier has won international recognition as one of America's foremost designers. She has since established fashion houses in Los Angeles, California, where she primarily works and lives, as well as in Manhattan's Upper East Side. She has designed the wedding dresses of the pop star Britney Spears and red carpet dresses for many Hollywood celebrities including Gwyneth Paltrow, Reese Witherspoon, Kristen Stewart, Jennifer Lopez, Taylor Swift, and Katy Perry. The daughter of Michel J. Lhuillier, a French-born Filipino businessman, and Filipina socialite-former model Amparito Llamas, Monique was raised and studied in Cebu City, attended the Fashion Institute of Design & Merchandising of St. Theresa's College in Manila, then continued her studies in Switzerland before moving to Los Angeles to pursue her fashion designing career. In 2003, Monique was invited for membership in the Council of Fashion Designers of America. In the Philippines, she was first awarded a "Medal of Honor" and later the "Presidential Medal of Merit" in 2006.

APL.DE.AP, 45. Allan Pineda Lindo, which is his real name, is a member of the Grammy award-winning American group The Black Eyed Peas. He was born in Angeles City in Pampanga to his Filipino mother, Cristina Pineda, who raised him as a single mother after his African-American father left the family shortly after his birth. Growing up with six younger siblings, Allan would take hour-long jeepney trips to and from his school to help his family farm sweet potatoes, corn, sugar cane, and rice. At age 14, with the help of a foundation for abandoned American children, Allan went to the United States for treatment of an eye problem. He was later adopted by Mr. Joe Hudgens and, living permanently in the U.S., started his singing career. Over the years, the Black Eyed Peas sold millions of their song albums with chart-topping songs, ranking 12th on the Billboard's Decade-End Chart Artist of the Decade and 7th in the Hot 100 Artists of the Decade. In 2019, Apl.de.ap collaborated with Filipino composer Ryan Cayabyab for his performance in the opening ceremony of the 2019 Southeast Asian Games in Manila.

REESE FERNANDEZ-RUIZ, 35. The president and founding partner of Rags2Riches, Inc., a social enterprise established in 2007, Reese along with her team have been helping women in poor communities in the Philippines to make a living from weaving eco-ethical fashion and home accessories. In 2015, Reese was recognized by *Forbes* magazine in its prestigious annual list of 30 "Under 30 Social Entrepreneurs," citing her as belonging to "an elite group of people who are directing their talent and conviction to better the world." Rags2Riches, which sells online and in retail stores a line of accessories created out of upcycled scrap cloth, organic materials, and indigenous fabrics, has trained 900 people in the business, mostly women who reside in one of the Philippines' biggest dump sites. Reese, who was born in the Philippines in 1985, was raised by her mother, a missionary who travelled and provided aid to the poor. It was her mother's work that exposed her to the poverty and suffering of people in the Philippines, inspiring her to pursue social entrepreneurship as her calling.

JOSE ROBERTO "ROBBIE" ANTONIO, 43. The founder and CEO of Resident Holdings Group, Robbie Antonio is a real estate developer, tech entrepreneur, and art patron. Recognized as a stalwart in consumer branding, he has worked with various celebrities and influencers for worldwide projects representing 20 companies in fields ranging widely from property and financial technology, to educational technology and e-commerce, to beauty and fashion, and to electronics and gaming. He is also the founder and CEO of Revolution Precrafted, a Manila-based modular building company established in 2015 that has supplied project designs for clients in the United States, Dubai, Myanmar, and the Caribbean. Robbie has a Master's in business administration from Stanford University and describes himself as a "deal-hungry" yet fair visionary who, instead of competing with other developers, partners and builds relationships with them with a win-win focus. He is also the managing director of Century Properties, a company established in 1986 by his father, the high-end real estate developer Jose E. B. Antonio who reshaped the Manila skyline with luxury branded buildings.

EMMANUEL (MANNY) PACQUIAO, 42. A Filipino boxer, actor, singer, endorser, politician, and successful entrepreneur, Manny Pacquiao is the first boxer to win major world titles in four of the eight "glamour divisions"—flyweight, featherweight, lightweight, and welterweight—and the only boxer to hold world championships across four decades—the 1990s, 2000s, 2010s, and 2020s. As of 2015, Pacquiao's 25 pay-per-view bouts had generated $1.2 billion in revenues, making him among the world's highest paid athletes. Manny parlayed his enormous success and popularity in boxing by going into politics, getting elected as a Philippine congressman and later winning as a senator that he still is today. Indeed, his is a truly remarkable rags-to-riches story. Coming from a very poor family in Mindanao, he quit high school and took to boxing bouts for pay in General Santos City to survive. By age 15 he got recognized as the best junior boxer in the southern Philippines, then sailed to Manila to continue his boxing training. He finally had his professional boxing debut in 1995 as a junior flyweight at age 16. Today, his net worth is estimated at $220 million.

HAPPY ANDRADA, 32. As a Filipina fashion designer, Happy Andrada has been making waves in the fashion world since graduating from the London's Central Saint Martin College Of Art And Design in 2012. That very same year, she won the "International Emerging Designer" award during the 2012 Miami International Fashion Week and later won two major awards in the 3rd Asian Weddings and Arts Competition in Hong Kong. Back in the Philippines three years later, in 2015, she won the "Smart Choice" award in the "Weaving the Future" competition held by the Fashion Design Council of the Philippines, during which she was also recognized as one of the year's "Inspiring Young Filipino Entrepreneurs." How did her fashion designs get such attention? Her designs are perennial show-stoppers because of her unique, complex detailing and her masterful use of material that has her personal brand seared on. Since then, Happy has participated in over 50 fashion shows worldwide, her heart for innovation and an ear that listens to her clients putting a smile on the faces of everyone who sees her work.

BRUNO MARS, 35. Peter Gene Hernandez in real life, Bruno Mars is a highly popular singer-songwriter, multi-instrumentalist, record producer, and choreographer. Mars became famous in 2010 with the release of the successful singles "Nothin' on You" by B.o.B and "Billionaire" by Travie McCoy, both of which featured his vocals. He has sold over 130 million records worldwide, making him one of the best-selling music artists of all time, and he has won several awards and nominations, including 11 Grammy Awards, three Brit Awards, nine American Music Awards, and 10 Soul Train Awards. Bruno grew up in a very musical family. His father, Pete, was a Latin percussionist from Brooklyn of half Puerto Rican and half Ashkenazi Jewish descent, and his mother, Bernadette San Pedro Bayot, is a singer who is half-Filipina with some Spanish ancestry who emigrated from the Philippines to Hawaii. Bruno struggled hard to make a breakthrough in the music industry, and with his strong determination began to find success by the early 2000s when he was commissioned to write songs for several popular artists in the U.S.

MICA TAN, 27. As president and CEO of the MFT Group of Companies, Mica Tan considers herself a pioneer in venture capital and angel investing where investors provide capital not only for entrepreneurial start-ups but also established businesses. She started MFT (the acronym of her name Maria Francesca Tan) in 2009 with three of her friends, all older than her, who were already involved in their individual businesses. Now, with assets of over US$61 million, MFT operates in nine countries and 18 cities worldwide. For this feat, Mica won the "Most Influential Filipina Award" in 2019 from the Filipina Women's Network. Running MFT though has not been without its challenges, but steadfastly refusing to focus on what others think or how they would judge her, she just keeps a sharp focus on achieving her business goals. She had developed her flair for business at an early age, already trading stocks at the Philippine Stock Exchange when she was only 13. By the time she was 15, she was already trading foreign exchange and being mentored by a renowned investor, all the while that she was working for the family's pawnshop business.

CHARICE PEMPENGCO, 28. When she was only 16, Charice Pempengco recorded herself singing the Dreamgirls anthem "And I Am Telling You I'm Not Going" then uploaded it on YouTube. The Ellen DeGeneres Show producers halfway across the world saw that clip that made them so spellbound that they promptly arranged to fly Charice from the Philippines to the U.S. to perform live on the show. In 2007, with web clips of her concerts garnering 15 million hits on YouTube, Charice found herself on the Oprah Winfrey Show, where her rendition of Whitney Houston's "I Have Nothing" brought the whole live audience to tears. Wowed, Oprah then introduced Charice to record producer David Foster, describing her to David as "the most talented girl in the world." They then worked together to produce her first U.S. single, "Note to God," which debuted in May that year on the Billboard Top 50. Since then, Charice has received over 35 awards worldwide—truly a remarkable feat for a little girl who had started out simply as a frequent contender in local amateur singing contests at the age of seven!(Charice acknowledged that she was male in 2017 and adopted Jake Cyrus as new performer name.)

NATASHA BAUTISTA, 23. A management graduate of the Ateneo de Manila University, Natasha Bautista used to be a runway model and member of the Professional Models Association of the Philippines. While doing a modeling engagement in Kuala Lumpur, Malaysia, she met the brains behind MyTeksi Malaysia and decided to join the team as an intern. Today, Natasha is now the acting general manager of GrabTaxi Philippines. She is known as a very hands-on leader, even conducting GrabCar orientations and trainings herself. Indeed, much of the success of GrabTaxi Philippines is credited to Natasha's keen understanding of its target market—working Filipino women like herself. Indeed, when she was named as the company's assistant general manager in 2015, she pushed for GrabTaxi cars to be painted with "pussy cabs" cartoon characters with three variants: "Sexy Fox," "Bipolar Panda," and "Mr. Moose." The cartoon characters caught a lot of media attention, and Natasha felt that this affirmed that cartoony cuteness is a valid business strategy in Asia. Even as AGM of GrabTaxi, Bautista moonlights every now and then as a professional model, gracing billboards in the Philippines and in runways across Southeast Asia.

CHAPTER 10

Maintain Your Enthusiasm and Your Positive Attitude

"Your life is your garden, your thoughts are the seeds. If your life isn't awesome, you've been watering the weeds."—
Terry Prince, owner, singer and songwriter

Consider the wisdom of Gen. Douglas MacArthur. The former commander of the U.S, Army's Southwest Pacific in World War II, the one who saved the Philippines from almost four years of Japanese occupation, Gen. MacArthur is credited to have said: "Years may wrinkle the skin, but the absence of enthusiasm wrinkles the soul."

True enough, you'd easily grow old fast if you constantly believe that terrible things will happen in any and everything you do. When you have a negative mental attitude, every time you hit a big snag the only things you'll see are closed and padlocked doors.

But if you're enthusiastic in everything you do, you won't see any closed doors ahead of you; instead, you'll see wide open gates with a wealth of good things and opportunities inside. When you instill hope and optimism in yourself, you'll be able to witness your own personal transformation before your very own eyes.

Have you ever experienced doing your job in the workplace and couldn't help but find yourself watching the clock in fitful waiting, waiting just for the day to be over?

If your answer is yes, you're a person with no "fire in your belly." That fire is your much-needed enthusiasm. You won't have it if you don't like what you're doing, if you don't have faith in your own ability, or if you fear failure in all the things you do.

Put it into your head that you won't be excited about doing something unless you have the great desire or passion to do it. If you force yourself to perform a job but don't have the desire to finish eagerly, you'd get bored. But if you're truly excited and motivated, you'd find yourself wanting to finish the task—not just finish the day—no matter how difficult the job might be.

When you do things that you believe you can do and do them well, that's self-confidence; however, when you do a task with optimism and your belly is on fire when you pursue your task despite obstacles that may come, that's enthusiasm.

In 2007, when I was the human resource director of one of the biggest universities in Cebu City, I conducted a group in-person interview for an instructor position. One applicant discussed a subject not in my line of my interest, but I was overly impressed and intrigued with his positive attitude. While talking about a teaching job experience in another university, he unknowingly shifted his discussion to his previous special study in the United States and how he coped with extreme weather condition there during winter.

He was beaming with coolness, so full of energy as he shared his story with the group. And his body language was electric, so full of enthusiasm that the other applicants listened to him spellbound, forgetting that their turn to be the next interviewee might come any time after him.

Indeed, at some level, we look at an enthusiastic person and think that what he's doing "Looks too good, looks great fun!" that we couldn't resist the urge to join in. This could make us think that "confidence is serious" and "enthusiasm is fun," thus making them spread like wildfire in your group.

We can compare enthusiasm to the fuel inside the tank of your car; it will take your car wherever you want to. But sometimes, you might wrongly load your thank with lower-grade or lower-performance fuel, making the car run too slow, do much less mileage, and get you horribly late to your destination.

During my younger days I involved myself in a lot of sports—softball, basketball, martial arts, and tennis. But when I started playing tennis I enjoyed playing it so much better that I gave up playing all the others. I find tennis very enjoyable, for it's a sport that you can continue to play even during your senior years and even long after your retirement.

My enthusiasm to play tennis got so strong that I seriously began training for and joining tennis tournaments at every opportunity. The big bonus for me in doing so was that every time I played competitive tennis, the rush of adrenalin would empty the anxiety and stress from my brain and I'd feel much better with myself—and get lots of energy going to work besides!

One doesn't have to be more skillful than the other person in order to succeed in a competitive undertaking like, say, sports or selling a product or service in the market. What it sometimes but not always takes is just a little more enthusiasm and motivation to win. And one thing is sure: When your mind is full of optimism and enthusiasm, you become unstoppable from pursuing your goal. This optimism-and-enthusiasm tandem surprisingly fuels your whole being with more power and greater endurance to attain your goal.

I'd like to share with you a common formula that I came across sometime ago for achieving great enthusiasm. It's the equation "E=mc."

No, of course it's not Albert Einstein's physics formula "$E=mc^2$", which means that the maximum atomic energy "E" that resides in a piece of matter is equal to its mass "m" multiplied by the speed of light squared.

More modestly but also immensely powerful, the formula "E=mc" means one's motivation "m" multiplied by one's courage "c." In short, your enthusiasm equals your willingness multiplied by your courage to act on what you want to achieve. The higher your "m" and your "c," so much better!

And here's one more thought—something of an energizing joke before we end this chapter—when stress happens to bring your enthusiasm down. You may have become "low-bat," so to speak, but don't despair and keep on smiling. The secret to revitalize yourself?

Give yourself a break if you feel STRESSED; enjoy some ice cream, chocolates, and cake. Why? It's because when you say the word STRESSED in reverse it becomes DESSERTS!

DESSERTS are something to savor and enjoy, aren't they?"

CHAPTER 11

Vanquish Your ANTs With Your APTs

*"Once you replace negative thoughts with positive ones, you'll start having positive results."—**Willie Hugh Nelson, American musician, actor, and activist (Born 1993)***

About an hour and a half past midnight of July 20, 2020, alone at home in Lapu-Lapu City in the island of Cebu, I woke up in overpowering panic. My throat was very sore and I felt shortness of breath that almost made me swoon. I rushed to the bathroom and gargled with warm salted water but couldn't taste the salt in it and I imagined that my sense of smell was also gone. Then this terrifying thought began pummeling my brain: "Oh my God, oh my God I must have contracted the Covid-19 virus!"

Shaking with fear, my mind raced with the idea of dying if I couldn't get myself to a hospital fast enough. But where and in what hospital could I go in that unholy hour, and how? Who will drive for me?

I felt so weak and so confused that I went back to bed and lay myself down. I prayed fervently in the silence of my room, after which I somehow remembered to do a simple breathing technique that I learned in high school and in college when I joined various martial arts clubs.

That simple meditation technique can be done by sitting down, or by laying yourself down on your bed if you want to sleep while meditating:

—Close your eyes just set your mind free;

—Inhale through your nose, and hold your breath for about 4 seconds;

—Exhale through your mouth, either focusing your sensation on the air coming in and out of your nose, or your sensation on the rise and fall of your chest, so that you won't generate thoughts coming into your mind.

I used this meditation technique during my college days when I arrived home after classes for just a 15-minute rest before going back to school to attend my dramatic guild's practice.

Also, one night in 1989 when I was working in Riyadh, Saudi Arabia, we celebrated a friend's birthday party and I was scheduled to join a karate tournament the following day and I had only two hours to sleep before the tournament. After meditating for 20 minutes I'd usually feel refreshed. That time, however, I began to feel relaxed and calm after only 15 minutes and fell fast asleep after that.

That severe panic attack that hit me in Lapu-Lapu City just a few months ago thankfully wasn't from having contracted the treacherous corona virus; a rigorous Covid-19 check later that day confirmed this. As I understand from my own readings of the medical literature, it was just typical of extreme negative thinking. We are all bound to suffer this kind of negativity attack at one time or another.

But why does it happen?

As neurologists explain it, the phenomenon of negative thinking happens in that part of our brain called the "amygdala," an almond-shaped mass of gray matter in its temporal lobe that functions as an alarm system, always on the lookout for danger, threats, and bad news.

Precisely to sound that alarm is the brain's default position, scientists believe.

Given this, the big question that can haunt us is this: "Can we possibly alter this default position of our brain?" The good news is "Yes, we can!" We can change that default system in our brain the way we can change the default system of our desktops or laptops. But how?

Simply by installing words of hope and positivity into that inner voice of ours.

As I mentioned earlier, that default setting of your brain automatically tells you that everything in life is difficult to achieve. Still, you don't have to listen and agree with that nonsense.

By an act of will, you can refuse your inner voice from planting the seeds of negativity and fear in your mind. Don't allow it to prevent you from starting from finding and seizing every new opportunity that comes in your life. Don't allow it to misdirect you and draw you away from the results that you desire.

Once you've installed the words HOPE and POSITIVITY to your inner voice, indeed once they have become the new default setting in your mind, you can truly watch your productivity multiply and your creativity rise many-fold!

The very thought-provoking acronym ANTs was coined for this achievement barrier in the 1990s by Dr. Daniel Amen, an American celebrity psychiatrist and brain disorder specialist who's also a five-time *New York Times* best-selling author. ANTs stand for "Automatic Negative Thoughts," thoughts that are so infected with negativity that you must kill them to put yourself back on the right track in your life.

At some point in our lives, all of us can harbor ANTs in the form of negative feelings and thoughts that foster low confidence and self-doubt in ourselves.

In 2001, when I was working as senior project support supervisor and later as executive secretary for a Saudi Aramco affiliate in the city of Al-Khobar, KSA, the general manager I reported to was an Arab national who'd give me very detailed and specific instructions in a voice so loud that I felt was very rude, insulting, and disrespectfully hurtful to those being addressed. That negative voice haunted and bothered me not only at work but even in my sleeping hours, making me uncontrollably mutter these incredulous questions to myself: "How could he? How dare he?"

Looking back to that time, I realize now that my thoughts at work had been full of ANTs—very harmful automatic negative thoughts against my Arab boss that, I eventually realized, he really didn't deserve to be their target.

In fact, only much later did I discover that his unpleasant loudness in giving orders to subordinates is normally and typically the managerial style of Arab nationals in their homeland. Ashamed of my ignorance, I then resolved to kill my ANTs, and in time was able to adjust and silence the voice of negativity in my head.

One other very important lesson I learned from that experience:

When employed overseas, you've got to clearly understand the culture and behavioral patterns of the country where you're working. Loudness and abrasiveness could just be a normal manifestation of that culture.

In the particular case of that boss of mine, he wasn't a bad person at all and actually had a soft spot in his heart. He'd invest time to talk and patiently explain work-related matters to subordinates, listen attentively to the suggestions of others, take pains to motivate staff to do their jobs and accomplish projects on time, and take the trouble to find ways to inspire us to be more productive at work.

On the subject of negativity that could fill our heads with ANTs, my daughter Sheena—she used to work as an assistant nurse head in Maryland in the United states but now works as senior nurse in a big call center in Cebu City—once shared this post on Facebook with a social media friend: "Don't treat negative people how they treat you. God hasn't called you to be a mirror reflecting the image and attitudes of others. He has called you to be a light shining in the darkness."

No matter how hopeless the situation, you can overturn it into a good outcome when you tame and transform your negative thoughts into positive ones. As is often said in times of crisis, there's no such thing as hopeless situations, only hopeless people. Indeed, if you embrace failure it would just attract more failure; but if you embrace success and celebrate it, more successes will definitely come to you.

Let me now end this chapter with these parting words:

Starting today, terminate the weeds of negativity in your brain; totally uproot them to prevent them from growing back to stunt your growth.

Don't believe the monster that lurks in your mind to continually try to stifle your enthusiasm and crush your optimism; instead, slay all the ANTs crawling inside your head so that all that remains there is only your APT—the automatic positive thoughts that will show you the way and lead you to your success!

CHAPTER 12

Get Out of Your Comfort Zone!

"You never change your life until you step out of your comfort zone; change begins at the end of your comfort zone."—**Roy T. Bennett, American thought leader, positivity and creativity advocate**

Do you have certain ways of doing things that you feel very comfortable doing even with your eyes closed? It won't be surprising if you do, for all of us each have our own unique sets of skills.

But to get out of your comfort zone and not doing those familiar ways could be a very uncomfortable and difficult process. You need to learn to adapt to the new ways that present themselves to you and to prove to be capable of doing them. It won't do for you to sing the same song every day and dance to the same music. You need to get out of the status quo every so often to discover and to do new and more exciting things that yields even better results.

How many times in your life have you done new and difficult things but you dismally failed? Maybe lots of times, after which you blamed yourself for doing something out of your comfort zone. This happens when you're always used to doing routine jobs in the past. This is when you've cultivated a mindset that looks at doing easy and routine tasks as most practical because there are little or no risks involved.

However, when you succeed in a confined and restrictive zone, you'll only have short-lived joy and won't experience the rewards from doing very fulfilling tasks. If this happens, your backtracked actions become a hindrance for you to achieve the life you deserve.

In his 2020 book *The Habit of Ferocity*, the leading American peak-performance expert Steven Kotler who's also a successful entrepreneur and *New York Times* bestselling author, declares: "In order to achieve peak performance you have to switch off mediocrity and switch on ferocity."

And what I love most in this book is Kotler's maverick advice on how to stay out of our comfort zone: "Be the best when you are at your worst." What he means by that is that when you dip yourself into new and even difficult situations, you'll be compelled to adapt to them as a matter of survival.

When pursuing your goals, you should never think that all you'd encounter is the proverbial bed of roses; most often, there could be lots of temporary setbacks and difficulties along the way. Realize that your comfort zone is a beautiful place to stay but hardly anything ever grows there; you need to know that success always begins with one step out of that comfort zone.

All the things that happen in our lives are products of either our positive or our negative outlook, which in turn is shaped by the thoughts that have been planted inside our mind. When you think negative, you become inactive; if you think positive, you can supplant your negativity with an inner forward moving force that will enable you to quickly accomplish your goal.

One of the most inspiring stories about the power of going out of one's comfort zone is the Biblical account of how the diminutive Hebrew shepherd David slew the Philistine giant Goliath: "When the giant of a man of the Philistines called Goliath boastfully challenged the best warrior of Israel and nobody would go forward, David fearlessly walked out of his comfort zone and boldly accepted the challenge." Drawing power from his faith in God, David killed Goliath despite the enormous difference in size between them.

Ferocity in dealing with life's adversities is not enough, however; you also need to have a good life work balance to overcome those adversities. I came to realize the importance of a good life work balance some years back when I made a firm resolve to improve my performance in competitive tennis.

At that time my long-held routine was to work from morning till afternoon, then play tennis at night. I tried very hard but failed to break the habit. But when I finally realized that an early morning exercise is the best time for the body to do physical activities, I decisively changed my routine—I started waking up at 4:00 A.M. instead so I could play my first tennis game by 5:30 A.M.

I found it very hard to adjust to my new routine, but I persisted until I started reaping positive results from the effort. Soon, once I've played at 5:30 A.M., a strong sense of well-being would come over me. I'd experience a renewed burst of energy in the workplace that made me much more productive.

Let me now share with you the 12 specific ways that I learned and practiced over the years to help me get out of my comfort zone. I have adapted them from the available success literature, which recommends ways ranging in number from 10 to 12. I've decided to stick to the 12 and I'm now presenting them below:

12 SPECIFIC STRATEGIES TO HELP YOU GET OUT OF YOUR COMFORT ZONE

1. **Envision a positive outcome.** If you're in darkness you wouldn't want to move out, but if you see brightness ahead you'd be motivated to move forward.
2. **Plan everything you do.** Chart out how you'd approach your goals in life. If you have a concrete plan, you could predict how you're going to achieve the things you dream of doing.
3. **Express gratitude.** When you are grateful of the things you have, you'll take advantage of every opportunity that comes along by doing the needed tasks right away.
4. **Know what you're into.** Obtain more information on what you're doing so you'll know in advance how to handle it and execute the needed action.
5. **Be friendly even in a hostile environment.** You'll survive if you'd still emerge as your calm self after mingling with antagonistic people. No matter what you do, always make an effort to meet and mingle even with such people; you can't just choose to associate with those whom you think are friendly. You have to establish harmonious relationships with all types of people in your workplace.

6. **Try to listen to music you don't like.** You can change your emotional make up by constantly exposing yourself to things you aren't very familiar with. Listening to music you don't like, for example, can help develop your brain to adapt more quickly to new environments.

7. **Try not to open your Facebook for two weeks.** Social media is a time-killer and can make you unproductive. Try to control your urge by avoiding it for some time.

8. **Make people happy in unusual ways.** Give flowers to your loved ones even if there are no important occasions or events. Surprises trigger good mood emotional feelings.

9. **Donate things you don't need.** Instead of storing things you don't really need nor don't need any more, try donating them to others. When you make people happy, you'll also feel happy.

10. **Practice meditation.** Scientific studies have found that meditation reduces negativity, bias, stress, and anxiety.

11. **Don't be afraid to take risks.** When you take calculated risks on the things you love to do, you'll feel challenged because it's a human instinct to survive, and as they say, when you survive you'll most likely also thrive.

12. **Accept difficult projects.** There's a military code that says "Do as you're told and complain later." When your boss or associates ask you to do a difficult task, it means that they believe in your skills and capabilities. Instead of doubting that you can do the job, accept it with self-confidence because such opportunities to prove yourself capable don't come very often.

So now it's time to move out of your safety nets, because real growth doesn't come from just hanging on to your comfort zone.

CHAPTER 13

Create Consistent, Good Daily Rituals

*"We are what we repeatedly do. Excellence then
is not an act, but a habit."—**Aristotle,
Greek philosopher and polymath
(385-323 BC)***

When you have certain habits that truly serve your purpose, the probability of you sticking to them would be high.Those good habits are of two types: *conscious habits*, those that you do intentionally; and *subconscious habits*, those that you may not even be aware of.

These good habits can help you make great progress in life, in sharp contrast to bad habits that can get you stuck, that can trap you relentlessly in a state of boredom, and that can prevent you from moving forward to your goals.

So, which of the two types of good habits do you have?

To fulfill your life's goals, you obviously would want to cultivate and retain both your good conscious habits and get rid of all your good subconscious ones. Whether good or bad, however, it won't be easy to change your habits because that would require a major shift in your behavior. Acquiring good habits can take some doing but not difficult to achieve, but really bad habits, like heavy smoking and inveterate alcohol drinking, are notoriously tough to get rid of.

From my copious readings of self-help books I learned this very educational lesson about habit: "**Habit is the junction of knowledge** ("What you want to do"), **skills** ("How you want to do it"), **desire** ("Your determination to do it"), **and the purpose** ("Why you will do it")."

Have you ever experienced doing something deeply personal in your life that threw you off the track? If yes, it must have derailed your strong commitment to a daily habit that was consistently moving you forward to an important goal.

I must admit—not without a stab of shame in my gut—that I went to so much struggle to get this book of mine written. The reason is that I used to be a chronic procrastinator. Until my later years I didn't follow a consistent daily routine. For sheer lack of commitment and engagement to anything important in my personal life, I wasted too much of my time and energy in doing countless trivial activities that I am loath to enumerate here.

When I came back to the Philippines for good in 2004, having finished and not renewed my contract as executive secretary and senior project support supervisor for a Saudi Aramco affiliate in Al-Khobar, KSA, my mind was endlessly badgered by the thought that I still couldn't start writing the book I had long dreamed of writing.

The excuse that I gave myself was that there was just too much distraction in my hometown in Cebu. I then decided to go to the United States, making a pledge to myself that I'd finally write the book there, but alas! I was unable to write even just the opening lines for it after five long months.

So back to the Philippines I flew! Still, I didn't get in the mood to start writing the book, so I decided to make myself productive in the interim by engaging in some income-generating activity.

I took a part-time teaching job in the MBA program at the University of the Philippines-Cebu and in the ETEEAP Program—that's the acronym for "Expanded Tertiary Education Equivalency and Accreditation Program"—at the University of San Jose Recoletos in Cebu City (both universities are my Alma Maters).

By teaching with only a light subject load, I had hoped to set aside some of my free time in writing, but to no avail. I got addicted to inconsequential things like watching Netflix, making endless chats and posts on Facebook, and other unproductive engagements that took so much of my time, attention, and energy. In fact, not even once during that whole semester was I able to write a single word for my book.

So with a desperate self-resolution to change my mindset in a more conducive, stress-free environment, I flew to the United States again in

March 2018 for our annual Cabahug family reunion in Texas. (I can see that you might now be quizzical how I can afford to do all that foreign travel, so I'll tell you now: I'm usually able to fly to Texas every year thanks to a free round trip Manila-Texas plane ticket sponsored by a family member.)

That time in 2018 I was gratified to have gotten my nerves back, and my will to write the book had returned. This enabled me to fast-track my writing. At last, I finally found my natural energy, enthusiasm, and regimen to finish the first draft of my book's manuscript.

It definitely isn't easy to accomplish major productive rituals like writing a book about something you're passionate about. However, I think you can likewise do it as I have done if you can just muster the motivation, the will power, and the burst of energy to take that small but decisive step of moving forward to achieve something that you're sure will truly change your life.

When in doubt about your capacity to reach your big life goals, just remember the wisdom of this saying: **"There are always two pains in life: the pain of discipline and the pain of regret."**

It's never too late to start developing healthy personal habits that are perfectly aligned with your fondest goals in life.

CHAPTER 14

Overcome Challenges, Obstacles to Your Path

"If you find a path with no obstacles, it probably doesn't lead anywhere."—Frank A. Clark, American lawyer and politician known for his thoughtful words of wisdom (1860-1936)

As the sagely saying goes, "Life is 10% of what happens to you and 90% of how you respond to it." This means that life is not what you take of it, but what you make of it. We cannot change our fate, but we can change the melody of our own life's music.

Another way to say that is this: How your life will go is all a matter of directing our own attitude. Life isn't what happens to you, but how you react to what happens to you.

In 1997, I put up a catering business in Cebu that was financed by my savings from my Middle East work engagements. The single-proprietorship outfit sold packed lunch to the staff of some 25 banks in the cities of Cebu, Mandaue, and Lapu-Lapu. We had several competitors in the business but we managed to make a sustained tidy profit.

But when the Asian financial crisis struck later in 1997, inflation rose so high that all of our competitors scrambled to raise their prices as a matter of survival. By that time I had gone back to the Middle East and was already in the middle of my contractual engagement as human resource and adminstration project head of a consultancy form servicing Saudi Aramco in Jeddah, Saudi Arabia. In my absence, I had arranged for my family in Cebu to run the catering business.

In my working station in Jeddah, I realized that I could lose the loyal customers of my catering business if I did the same thing of increasing prices as our competitors had done. Rather than increase prices, I decided to be contrarian by instructing my family to even lower our prices by 25 centavos (that's one-fourth of the Philippine peso).

That price reduction was coupled with this three-pronged operational strategy:

First, I arranged to open a saving account in each of my customer banks in Cebu and offered to give each of the bank managers a 50% discount on their food orders but with this proviso—that that they'd collect the payments of their bank staff for their food orders, then deposit them directly to that savings account of ours every 15th and 30th of the month;

Second, we gave a free diet regimen to each of our clients in the participating banks;

And third and last, we inscribed the name of each of our bank customers on their respective lunch boxes as a form of assurance that they'd be the only users of their respective lunch boxes.

The happy result was that despite the severe economic crunch brought by the Asian financial crisis, our food catering business bounced back to good financial shape and gained even more loyal customers.

Indeed, obstacles are the landmines standing between you and your goals, but your ability to overcome these obstacles is what will make you different from your competitors or with people similarly situated.

When hit by intimidating or suffocating difficulties in life, don't give up so easily. Just focus on your vision and believe in yourself. You might not be able to control the situation as it comes, but you can control your mindset and your actions towards it.

Let me tell you a deeply personal story about surmounting serious obstacles in one's life.

In 2010, while working at the Bahrain Training Institute that is run by the Kingdom of Bahrain's Ministry of Education, I got seriously ill with the measles. I suffered very high fever and severe stomach pains that terribly exacerbated my ulcer symptoms.

In bed in my apartment in the hot gulf city of Manama in Bahrain, there was even a time when I slept too long that it felt like eternity; bad dreams swirled in my unconscious mind all throughout that time.

And when I finally woke up, I discovered to my horror that I had slept straight for more than a day—exactly 26 hours, in fact!

In those fearful moments, my anxiety rose to a fever pitch with the thought of my possibly dying all alone in a foreign land. It was only when I did what seemed like a superhuman, almost miraculous exertion that I got back to my feet, wriggling from bed and staggering out of the bedroom dazed but deliriously happy that I was still alive!

I profusely thanked The Almighty for my recovery! After that heartbreaking health crisis, however, my self-confidence and self-worth sunk very low indeed. It took me all of 19 days to feel really well and fit enough to resume my teaching at the Bahrain Training Institute. I was greatly determined to do so, for I was fixated on reaching my goal of getting at least a one-year teaching experience abroad.

As it turned out, not only was I able to successfully conquer that major health setback; I even exceeded that goal, notching a teaching stint of as many as four years in the Middle East!

My point here is that wherever you are and in whatever adverse situation you might be, you must have the courage of breaking through whatever barriers get thrown across your way in your pursuit of your goals.

As I was writing this chapter, I was reminded of the ancient story about a young man who asked Greek philosopher Socrates this question: "What, Master, is the secret to success?"

Socrates looked at the young man with a straight face but gave no answer. Instead, he told him to meet him near the river the next morning.

When they met that morning, Socrates asked the young man to walk with him across—*not along*—the river. The young man dutifully obeyed. When they reached the point where the water got up to their necks, Socrates surprised him by dunking him into the water.

The shocked young man struggled to get out of the water, but Socrates steadily kept him submerged until he started turning blue. Ultimately, Socrates pulled the young man's head out of the water to keep him from drowning.

As the young man gasped and was taking deep breaths of air,

Socrates nonchalantly asked him: "What did you want the most when you were there?"

"Air," the boy replied.

Then Socrates said calmly: "That is the secret to success, young man. When you want success as badly as you wanted the air, then you will get it; there is no other secret."

To conclude this chapter, I now would like to share with you my 12-step recommendation for dealing with barriers to the achievement of your goals.

THE 12 STEPS FOR OVERCOMING MAJOR CHALLENGES AND OBSTACLES

1. **Tame your fear.** When you allow fear to overshadow you, the more you won't meet head-on the problem you're facing and you'll just quit. We all have temporary setbacks but they can make you fail only when you're afraid to get over the hump.
2. **Focus on your goal.** When you have no clear goal, many unexpected obstacles and setbacks will get in your way. Remember that there are things that you can do, actions that you can take, and decisions that you can make to help you implement the action part of your goals.
3. **Acknowledge your condition.** Sometimes when confronted with adversity, we tend to lose our self-worth so before taking action, we comfortably stay in our denial mood much longer than necessary.
4. **Be aware of yourself.** Sometimes obstacles are just a product of your fertile imagination. If you fully understand and are aware of your capability, you can quickly differentiate real obstacles from a simple setback and move forward without delay.
5. **Understand the struggle of successful people.** When you see someone successfully overcome obstacles that are heavyweight compared to yours, you'll find it easier to confront and handle your problems.

6. **Be willing to take a calculated risk.** When you take risks to solve your problems, you'll enhance your emotional intelligence and be able to use it to help you tackle the hardship that you're experiencing. Taking risks is a form of bravery and it's all we really need to face anything that life throws on us.

7. **Believe in yourself.** Widen your perspective of the situation you're in; this will greatly help you in establishing your self-confidence to overcome obstacles. When you have strong self-belief, it's as if you can do anything in life.

8. **Control your emotions.** When you're engulfed with too much emotion, you can't be objective enough to see the logic of a major setback, thus making you lose control of the situation. Too much emotion will hamper your decision-making, so make an effort to control it.

9. **Seek the support of others.** Don't hesitate to enlist the help of others who have the expertise to help you solve your problems. Sometimes the response we need to solve our difficulties can only be found outside ourselves.

10. **Be proactive not reactive.** When you anticipate what will happen in the future, the better will you be prepared. But when you just react to something, the bigger the obstacles will become.

11. **List your priorities.** When you write down what's bothering your mind and what your feelings and the possible solutions are, the more you'd be inclined to act immediately as you'd be better able to see light at the end of the tunnel, so to speak.

12. **Never give up.** If there's no pain there's no gain. To reach your pinnacle of success, don't ever lose hope and courage to stand up and continue the journey.

In sum, my firm advice when you're faced with big challenges in your work or major involvements: Do all of the 12 steps listed above without missing even a single step!

CHAPTER 15

Learn from Your Life's Experiences and from Those of Other People

> *"Experience is simply the name we give to our mistakes."*—**Oscar Wilde, popular**
> **Irish poet and playwright**
> **(1854-1900)**

We know it in our hearts that our own experiences could teach us how to improve our own life and our personal decision-making, but we have to admit that far better teachers in this respect are the inspiring experiences of self-made people, particularly those who have achieved remarkable success after failing not just once or twice before attaining it.

We look up to them and to their achievements—and of course to how they bounced back from their mistakes—as guideposts for making ourselves the best we can be in our own careers or callings.

In the early 1990s, while working in the Middle East as a human resource and administration project head for an oil company, I learned a very valuable and unforgettable lesson about committing mistakes.

In those days, every time I fumbled or made an error in my work I'd always come up with a perfect excuse to defend myself. My ego gave me the distorted perception that I should be nothing less than perfect in my job. For this reason, I always made it point to try to avoid any negative mark in my superiors' evaluation of my job performance. Eventually, however, I observed something very surprising in the workplace that gave me pause.

When they committed mistakes, our American top managers—including the CEO himself—would invariably admit those mistakes and always took accountability for them. My own immediate boss who was the company's vice president, on many instances after making even the slightest mistake, would apologize to me by saying "Oh sorry about that Archie!"

To be honest, given my wrong mindset and sense of values at that time, I found it incredible that an executive of such high rank would embarrass himself by apologizing to a subordinate like me way below his rank. That made me realize that if I wanted to move up in my career, I needed to make a drastic attitudinal change—that henceforth, I should take full responsibility and accountability for my actions at all times.

My perception about the reality in workplace relationships drastically changed because of that experience!

Outside the workplace, of course, a great source of instructive life experiences are our own parents. They are our very first teachers in our life and as we grow, we continue to be guided by the lessons they had imparted to us.

From my Dad Alberto Cabahug, who didn't even finish college but became an astute businessman and a Mandaue City councilor, I'd already learned a few things about the ropes of doing business when I was only age nine—things like salaries, labor unions, pickets, and employee walkouts.

This was because among the properties that Dad owned, had put up, or had acquired during his lifetime were a one-hectare lot in Lo-oc, Mandaue City, with old tiles as flooring that stored seawater daily that was left it to dry into salt, which was then stored in a warehouse; fishponds spanning about one hectare in the city's Lo-oc District; and, from the 1950s to the 1990s, a peanut plantation in Lapu-Lapu City with a work force of 20. In his later years my Dad also became a philanthropist who'd make donations to charitable foundations and other worthwhile causes.

Around every third week of December in those days, Dad would hand to me a large bunch of cash that I'd stuff into Christmas gift envelopes for his company staff and workers. By the 22nd—three days before Christmas Day—I'd distribute those gift envelopes to their recipients at the end of the day's working hours.

I remember that I did the same ritual every Christmas season, putting gift money inside envelops that the Cabahug family members and I would distribute to kids in our Lapu-Lapu City neighborhood.

In 1973, however, Dad unfortunately died intestate at the age of 88 when I was only in my second year in high school. He left behind all of his properties without first dividing them among his family beneficiaries—his five children from his first wife Perpetua, and me and my sister Linda from his second wife, our Mom Juliana.

This got me and Linda in a very prolonged court litigation from 1975-2018—a total of 43 years!—before we could get our fair share. In fact, after graduating from college in 1981, and considering that she was a real estate broker, Linda was appointed by the court to be the administrator for all of my father's properties.

The great lesson I learned from this family tragedy is that as a father, I need to make sure that all of my children are accorded their rightful inheritance while I'm still living; doing so will spare them from the most unfortunate and very inconvenient legal entanglement that's still happening to me and my sister even as I was writing this book, forcing her and me to go through the big hassle of making court appearances every so often.

Once we get more mature, we'd gain a wider wealth of experience in life as well as greater maturity in our outlook. And I must add that growing older shouldn't be cause for regret, as it's a privilege enjoyed only by some but denied to many.

In any case, we should never underestimate the value to us of other people's experiences, which as I pointed out at the outset could be far better teachers than our own experiences in helping us avoid mistakes in decision-making.

The motivational expert and author Bryan Golden summed up very strongly and much more pointedly the value of other people's experiences: "Don't waste time learning from your own experiences. Acquire an edge by learning from what others have already been through. Whatever your goals may be, there are those who have a lot to teach you because they have already traveled your path."

CHAPTER 16

Conquer the Tendency To Procrastinate

"Never put off till tomorrow what you can do today."
—Thomas Jefferson, American statesman,
diplomat, lawyer, architect, philosopher, and
and Founding Father who served as third
presidentof the United States of America
(1743-1826)

One Friday night in 2004 in Al-Khobar, Saudi Arabia, I woke up from my deep sleep when I remembered with a jolt that I absolutely had to submit an important written assignment to my boss the following day. The task wasn't really a complicated one but I negligently sat on it, not even giving it a thought from Thursday till Friday that week believing that I could finish it quickly anytime anyway.

Silently cursing myself for not doing it right away, I worked furiously like a madman to finish the document before the 7:00 A.M. Saturday deadline. I managed to finish it but barely met the deadline for its submission, for I still had to do a 30-minute drive to the office of my boss in the oil company's headquarters 20 miles away.

"Whew!" was all I could say to myself when it was all over.

If you've been in this horrible situation one time or another, don't feel so bad anymore because now you've learned from me that you're not alone. You and I are now two certified members of "The Dilatory Club"—the association of people guilty of the cardinal sin of procrastination.

Procrastination is like a big sinkhole that many of us continue to fall into despite knowing precisely where it's located so it won't give us a jolt the next time around. Indeed, scientific studies that looked into this problem have found out that 95% of people procrastinate to some degree.

Come to think of it, it's scary and sobering to realize just how much procrastination can hold us back from doing our jobs well and from advancing in our respective organizations and in our personal lives as well.

Do you know exactly why people procrastinate?

Some people think procrastination is a form of laziness, but it's a much deeper problem than that. *Laziness* means doing nothing or it'sthe unwillingness to act on something whether important or unimportant. In contrast, *procrastination* is the act of doing something more enjoyable rather than doing an unpleasant but more important task.

People who procrastinate have a wrong understanding of the meaning of time. They think they'll more have time to get something done when the right time comes, so they'll wait and wait but as it often happens, that right time never comes for them.

Habitual procrastinators not only become unproductive but eventually lose enthusiasm. This is an outcome that can lead to a sense of hopelessness and even the loss of their jobs. The lack of self-control and discipline of procrastinators can make them fall apart, unable to see an opportunity when it comes or to seize the moment for their advantage.

This is why procrastination is often called "an opportunity assassin."

Seriousness aside for a moment, I think you'll love the joke cracked sometime ago by English actor and television presenter Christopher Parker about that detestable habit. "Procrastination is the thief of time," he said. "It is like a credit card: it's a lot of fun until you get the bill."

So then, to help us decisively overcome or wean ourselves from the habit of procrastination, I'd like to share with you now the following 10 action steps that have all been proven effective for combating it:

10 ACTION STEPS FOR COMBATING PROCRASTINATION

1. **Accept that you procrastinate.** You can't change what you don't accept. This is honesty to oneself and is part of being accountable.

2. **See the outcome of the task, not the process.** Envisioning the positive results of what you're doing can motivate and encourage you to continue doing your task.

3. **Start a simple task.** When people are faced with difficult task, they might feel intimidated and stop. Some self-help books suggest that doing the hard task first is better when your brain isn't fatigued yet, thus making you much less likely to give up or procrastinate.

   But doing the simple tasks first can help us broaden our insights. And the more we gain insights, the more we can motivate ourselves to finish the task. It's just like seeing the light inside the tunnel; you need to hurry up before the brightness disappears.

4. **Do not allow distractions to interfere your work.** One of the time-tested distractions of our current generation is the overuse of social media or overindulgence in them. They can give you instant gratification but you have to control and discipline yourself. Use social media only as a form of reward when you've already finished doing your must-do tasks.

5. **Give yourself a treat.** Research shows the human brain responds to reward stimulus and this can be a good way to create habits. If you love espresso macchiato but seldom drink it, for instance, try gifting yourself with it after accomplishing a difficult task on time.

   Try putting a picture of the espresso macchiato on your to-do lists. We are visual human beings, so anything we see and like stimulates us to do more.

6. **Strike the iron while it's still hot.** Start a task immediately while you're still motivated. When you're distracted, you can lose the enthusiasm to do the task. The moment the iron

becomes cold it will harden, and the opportunity to make an excellent shape out of it gets lost.

7. **Cultivate self-confidence.** When you gain self-confidence you become a better person, happy, and free from fear because you've come to believe in your capabilities.

8. **Listen to music.** Scientific studies have shown that music produces several positive effects on the human body and brain. Music activates both the left brain and right brain at the same time, and the activation of both hemispheres can maximize learning and improve memory. If your memory improves, you'll surely generate more ideas.

9. **Have a very clear objective.** When you've got a clear sense of purpose in your life, the more you'll be inclined to do your assigned tasks sooner.

10. **Make a firm commitment.** One reason why you procrastinate is likely that the task doesn't meet your core values. Just be sure to do only tasks that are in accordance with your belief system.

Procrastination is something that you can't completely keep away from, but becoming mindful of the reasons why you procrastinate and how to conquer those tendencies may help you conquer your procrastination permanently.

CHAPTER 17

Don't Ever Let Failure Stop You!

"The greatest glory in living lies not in never falling, but in rising every time we fall."—**Nelson R. Mandela, South African anti-apartheid revolutionary, philanthropist, and South Africa's president from 1994 to 1999 (1918-2013)**

Sometime ago I came across this very interesting story from the American social news aggregation site *Reddit*:

"As my friend was passing the elephants, he suddenly stopped, confused by the fact that these huge creatures were being held by only a small rope tied to their front leg. No chains, no cages. It was obvious that the elephants could at any time break away from the ropes they were tied to, but for some reason they did not.

"My friend saw a trainer nearby and asked why these beautiful, magnificent animals just stood there and made no attempt to get away.

"Well," he said, "when they are very young and much smaller, we'd use the same size rope to tie them and, at that age, it's enough to hold them. As they grow up, they are conditioned to believe they cannot break away. They believe the rope can still hold them, so they never try to break free."

So the ability of those powerful and gigantic creatures to walk freely had been permanently impaired by a limitation imposed on them in the past by their puny human trainers—and only with a small rope tied to a front leg!

Like those elephants, we'd have our minds forever incarcerated inside a very small confined zone simply because we were made to believe that we couldn't do something so basic to our very own nature. In short, we'd be unable to do something because of our fear to do it!

In 2012, when I began my obligatory annual ritual of going to the

United States and living there for a few months, one of the things I hated so much was winter time. Staying for a family reunion in Ingram, Texas, where it seldom snows but is actually too cold, I always suffered too much pain in my body. So fearful was I of getting frozen stiff that I couldn't do anything productive.

After one such terrifying bout with the winter season, I made it a point to always plan my U.S. trip in time for summer. Still, there were times when it became absolutely obligatory for me to be in the U.S. in winter—a situation that gave me no choice but to seize the bull by its horns, so to speak.

One of the things I learned in my HR practice is the wisdom of this adage: "We have no control of the situation, but we have control on how to deal with it."

So, to tame my fear at that time, I practiced mind-conditioning to a high degree. With all my might I strongly instilled in my brain the idea that dealing with the discomforts of the winter cold is much more preferable than dealing with the constant, enervating humidity in the Philippines.

Indeed, I finally overcame the terror of the winter cold by engaging in some very rigorous indoor physical activities like doing early morning push-ups, practicing my nonchucks (chainstick) and *arnis* stick, set-ups, punching my *makiwara* board, and playing tennis three times a week even at 0 degrees Centigrade. They enabled me to adapt to the cold to such a level that my personal work productivity even increased.

Lee Colan, an American leadership consultant and author of the best-selling book *The Power of Positive Coaching*, came up with a very apt acronym for the dreaded word "fear."

To Colan, who is a cofounder of L Group Consulting, the word "FEAR" stands for "**F**alse **E**vidence **A**ppearing **R**eal," which he says succinctly describes how our minds can weave together false tales for how situations will turn out.

Since fear is often false or not true, Colan argues, you should be wary of falsehoods and shouldn't let it sink deeply into your mind. When you do this, once you experience the first pang of failure and you start believing that it's for real, then you'll always be afraid to stand up and make an effort to overcome it.

Then Colan came up with another acronym for FEAR that we should fiercely resist if we want to succeed in life. It's "FEAR" for "**F**orget **E**verything **A**nd **R**un."

Neither should we run away while doing something because of fear based on false evidence, and nor should we be so fearful of starting something because of our fear of not doing it right.

I'd say I had no such fear when right after graduating with my B.S. in Commerce in Cebu City in 1981, I started a handicraft business supplying a number of exporters with a line of coconut-shell and seashell fashion accessories. The business was doing very well but when I accepted an overseas job in the Middle East in 1985, I entrusted the business to a trusted close friend who had helped me set it up; just a few months after I left for abroad, however, the business floundered so miserably that I had it closed down for good.

Later, during lulls in my intermittent Middle East contractual engagements from 1993 to 2014, I would open and close down three more businesses:

—A successful lunch catering service to various banks in Cebu City, Lapu-Lapu City, and Mandaue City. (It likewise floundered when my former employer in the Middle East invited me to rejoin the firm and I had to ask relatives to run the lunch catering service in my absence.);

—A management consulting firm in Valenzuela City, Metro Manila that didn't last long for lack of clients. (I was a newcomer in Metro Manila and had no network of people to start with.); and

—A franchised dumpling business (baked dessert wrapped in dough) in Caloocan City that I had to shelve temporarily when I was beseeched by my my son, Keene to attend a very urgent matter in the United States. (I stopped the dumpling business for good because the external business landscape by then had taken a turn for the worse).

The very valuable lesson that I learned from these four aborted business startups is simple: When you venture into any business, you can't run it *in absentia*; you should be "hands-on" at all times because you can't expect your friends and relatives to have the same passion and commitment to its success as yours.

You can be sure than when the going gets rough for that business, those running it for you in proxy will cower in fear of failure when obstacles and problems start buffeting it and threatening to bring it down to the ground.

CHAPTER 18

The Need to Choose The Right Companions

""You are the average of the five people you spend the most time with."—Emanuel James Rohn (Jim Rohn)American entrepreneur, author, and motivational speaker (1930-2009)

Having harmonious relationships with others is one of the reasons why some people are happy and are able to achieve their life's goals. Imagine having to work all your life alone. Is that even possible?

Of course not; we are social creatures who need to interact with other people to fruitfully live our lives. We have no choice but to do so because otherwise, our constant companions would be the sun during the day, the moon at night, or perhaps our pet dogs or cats during all those hours when we are awake at home.

To maintain friendly relationships with our fellow humans is like mountain-climbing. It will either bring us up or take us down. Some friends will keep you down in the valley always because they couldn't sustain the effort to climb with you to the mountaintop.

If you associate yourself with the right people, both of you could go up to the summit, but if you choose the wrong companion, he or she will just pull you down. And like everybody else, when your supposed friend brings you down, you'll be in for big, big trouble.

You better believe it that when you hang out with positive-minded people, you'll invariably develop a positive outlook in life. This is because otherwise, if you spend a lot of time with people who see only the bad side of things, your mindset will surely be infected by their negativity and pessimism. You'll end up with a dark, sordid, and devastating view of life.

Ask yourself this question: Precisely who are the people who shaped your life as you know it today? They are your friends, your colleagues, your coworkers, and of course the members of your own immediate family.

Whether you like it or not, they have greatly influenced how you think, how you see and feel things, how your values in life have taken shape. This is the very reason for choosing your friends and companions very carefully, for it certainly is no exaggeration to say that we—yes, we—*are* the company we keep.

I remember with dismay that in my adolescent years, I hanged out much too often with some basketball friends who were so unsportsmanlike that they couldn't help but look at our opponents in negative, disdainful ways. Their constant epithet of the day was either "I should have elbowed that guy!" or "Next time let's do some dirty tricks so they won't be able to get near the goal!"

The longer I hung out with such wrong kind of people, I noticed that I myself would increasingly become more critical of other people. This only stopped when I finally decided to call it quits mingling out with them.

Looking back, it's crystal-clear to me now that when you start developing your own core values, you'll find it harder to stay around with people who don't share those values with you.

In the 1960s, the Polish-American psychologist Solomon Asch conducted what he called the "Conformity Experiment." He designed the set of experiments to measure the degree to which a person's own opinions are influenced by the opinions of groups around that person.

Asch drew a vertical black line on a plain white card and asked different groups of volunteers to guess the length of that vertical black line. The results were fascinatingly instructive. Each person's guess of how long that vertical black line was, turned out to be dependent on the volunteers who surrounded them.

If the people surrounding them overestimated the length, the guessers did the same and overestimated it; conversely, if those same people around them underestimated that same length, they underestimated it likewise.

So, literally, the volunteer guessers saw the vertical black line differently depending on the people around them.

From those experiments, Asch concluded that to conform to the thinking of the rest of the group, people are willing to ignore reality and give an incorrect answer to the same question asked of them.

The study also showed that people apparently conform to either of two main types of influences.

The "normative influence" prevails when people want to fit in with the group, and the "informational influence" prevails when people believe the group is better informed than they are.

A corollary conclusion that we can draw from Asch's "Conformity Experiment" is that the right way to achieve your passion in life is to have a keen, strong awareness and self-control in choosing the persons you want to mingle with. You may not be able to control everything that happens to you, but you can control how to respond to what happens to you by picking the right course of action.

In the 1990s, when I was working in a multinational oil firm in the Middle East, I had a co-worker and close friend—let's just call him Jack to protect his privacy—who was very friendly but whose frame of mind was so overly pessimistic. He was the type of person who proverbially often sees a half-full glass of water as half-empty.

Some of our fellow staffers in the office studiously avoided him. I didn't do the same because I felt a pang of guilt thinking that if I did, it would be so unfair to him. I truly believed—and I still do today—that we have the responsibility to tell the truth to others especially if the persons concerned are close to you. I then decided to privately but very frankly talk to him about the bad perception of our colleagues regarding his negative attitude.

He took my gesture in a very positive manner and I was very happy that after a few months, all of us in the office began to observe a big change in his attitude. He became positive and enthusiastic—and friendlier.

Talking about skills development, it's highly advisable to associate with the right people whose skills are better than yours. In my case as a club tennis player, for example, I always make the effort to play against players in the higher skills level. This is because I believe that there are a lot of lessons to be learned from people who are better than I am.

I remember a particularly good tennis player that we had in the early 1990s in our tennis club at the Mactan Air Base in Cebu. A Philippine Air Force general, he gave me a handicap with a wager by using only his backhand. The condition was that he can only return my ball using his backhand; if he uses his forehand instead, that would be a point for me.

Even with the handicap he gave me, I'd still often lose the game— which, of course, meant that he often got my money. However, this didn't deter me from pursuing my goal to improve my tennis skills because I considered the wager-with-handicap as an investment for my self-improvement.

And the result? My lopsided matches with that Philippine Air Force general improved my tennis performance very much. In less than two months, I already managed to win over him. From that time onward we played regular singles—with him not giving me the handicap anymore.

Some people believe that cultivating friendships is jollier and more exciting when you're still young because you've got more energy to expend for the effort. However, mature people likewise gain an advantage and will benefit from having many friends.

According to a study conducted by the Flinder's University in Adelaide, Australia, older adults who have close confidants are likely to live longer. The study, which followed the lifestyles of 1,500 adult people for 10 years, discovered that those with a large network of friends outlived their counterparts by as much as 22%. The study also found that close friendships can help ward off depression and boost the older adults' immunity as well.

I will now conclude this chapter by offering my 12 benchmark attributes below for the kind of people with whom you can cultivate and enjoy long-lasting friendships:

THE 12 BENCHMARK ATTRIBUTES
OF PEOPLE TO DEVELOP
LONG-LASTING FRIENDSHIPS WITH

1. **Well-disciplined individual.** People who can't resist temptations lack discipline. Choose well-disciplined companions because they can be great influencers. A 2013 study published in *Psychological Science* reports that "when people are running low on self-control, they often seek out self-disciplined people to boost their willpower."

2. **Good motivator.** People who get out of their way to push you to reach your goals are genuine friends. When you have a companion who encourages you a lot, you'll most likely also become like them and then you can build each other up.

3. **An inspiration.** The people whose works and accomplishments inspired you would be good role models. Just ensure that when they become your friends, they'd also be genuinely interested in what you're doing.

4. **Who share the same values you have.** To be with somebody whom you share the same values means you show respect for each other's actions because those values are within the bounds of your belief system. You're both willing to be held responsible and accountable in everything you do.

5. **Similar hobby as yours.** Every time you see a person with the same hobby, you'd become happy and excited just with the thought of the two of you having fun together. You'd want to go out with him or her and enjoy, say, swimming, playing tennis, listening to rock music, or simply going out for a relaxing walk.

6. **Not jealous of your success.** A friend who's envious of your success means they only think of their own selfish pursuits in life. Choose a friend who will support you to achieve your goal.

7. **Interested to gain knowledge.** Try to keep friends who are hungry for knowledge because they'll push you out of your

comfort zone to learn more things in life. Keeping them will expand your mindset and expose you to greater things.

8. **Honest.** When a friend tells you things with brutal honesty you can always trust what they tell you, even if it hurts. Genuine friends will tell you what you need to hear rather than what you like to hear.

9. **Good adviser.** A friend's advice can open your eyes to reality and enlarge your perspective. If one of you falls, the other can help the other get up.

10. **Optimistic person.** A toxic friend is a serious threat to your happiness. Avoid negative influences by hanging out only with positive-minded individuals as they can offer you plenty of positive reinforcement.

11. **A cool-headed companion.** Avoid bad-tempered companions; otherwise you'll learn their ways and become a hot-headed individual yourself.

12. **Good supporter.** Friends usually enjoy so much during fun times, but the right and good friend for you is one who will stand by you when things get tough. These are people who understand that life does not always follow the path you plan. They will provide you with a good motivation to do your thing.

Summing up, to achieve phenomenal growth in your career and in your life as a whole, you need as much as possible to surround yourself with friends who are smarter, better, and faster than you are or you could ever hope to be.

CHAPTER 19

To Grow, You Must Learn to Forgive

"The weak can never forgive. Forgiveness is the attribute of the strong."
—*Mohandas Karamchand Gandhi, Indian lawyer, anti-colonial
nationalist, political ethicist, nonviolent resistancecampaign
leader for India's independence from British rule
(1869-1948)*

When South African anti-apartheid revolutionary and political leader Nelson Mandela was elected president of South Africa in 1991, he specifically asked that his prison guards during his 27-year imprisonment as political prisoner be invited to attend his inaugural ceremony. When asked why he did that, Mandela replied that if those guards were not at the ceremony, he'd still be in prison because his mind would still be in chains.

Mandela had such an extraordinary character and frame of mind that instead of taking retribution when he rose to South Africa's presidency, he didn't allow vindictiveness to thrive in his heart. Forgiving to a fault, he refused to exact revenge on those who had done him grievous wrong before he rose to power.

How about you? Do you think that you can't ever forgive anyone who has done you a terrible wrong? Are you capable of overcoming the sense of vindictiveness in your heart, of giving a chance for your emotional wounds to heal, and of ultimately forgiving those who had inflicted those wrongs on you?

No matter how grievous the transgressions have been committed against you, you must be willing to eventually shake off the burden of hard feelings that you're carrying inside you. Allowing the feelings of bitterness to continually occupy a space in your heart and mind would certainly make you an emotional wreck; it would just needlessly sap your energy and enthusiasm to move forward in your life.

When I was working in a Middle East oil company in 1997, a colleague of mine did me something so terribly and unforgivably wrong.

What happened was this:

One day our King-Wilkinson office administrator in Al-Khobar, Saudi Arabia, instructed me to pick up an American coworker on my way to work from my apartment about 4 miles from our workplace in Jeddah. I knew that there was another guy in-charge of picking up that American coworker and driving him to office every day, but I was specifically ordered by a high-ranking manager to do it and so I did.

After picking up the American worker and driving him to his place of work, I proceeded to my office and found his regular assigned driver waiting for me. He was fuming mad at me for the faux pas.

"How dare you do that!" he repeatedly screamed at me. "You knew all along that I'm the one assigned to regularly pick up that American but you had the gall to do it yourself without letting me know. I waited for him so long but he was a no-show because you were such a lousy do-gooder!"

Shocked by his unrestrained rage, I tried to explain that I got a very specific and precise instruction from our head office to pick up that American. But the irate guy just won't listen to me. He continued berating me so violently that I was on the verge of hitting him with a body blow.

At that point I realized that the confrontation might lead to very serious negative consequences, so I held back. I told him to call up our administrator who I said just wasn't able to coordinate with him about the change of plan about that pickup. I then left feeling so terribly disrespected and personally hurt by that guy's immaturity in going into such a violent rage against me.

Since that incident I came to dislike that person so intensely. I felt he had stepped over the line of civilized behavior. The emotional wound he had inflicted on me was just too deep and so terribly hurting that I put it in my mind never to forgive him.

I have been brought up by a devoted Roman Catholic family and educated in an exclusive Catholic school from elementary through 4th year high, so the act of forgiving had been deeply inculcated in me, and

I believed that forgiveness is the only way we could move on without carrying a heavy burden in our lives.

But that terrible incident made me think that forgiveness didn't apply to all situations, and that vengeance was the only way to get rid of that burden. Yes, to hit back, to inflict on the aggressor the same pain he or she had inflicted on us!

However, those thoughts of violent reprisal made me feel even more stressed out, angrier, more bitter. My negative thoughts made me lose focus on my work. I eventually realized that if I continued wasting my time finding ways to retaliate, I'd never be able to get rid of the heavy weight inside my heart and won't be able to move on.

I learned much later in real life that to be able to forgive, one has to clearly identify, fully feel, express deeply, and then release one's bitterness and pain. To forgive, one has to self-heal and to transform one's anger and loathing into forgiveness.

You have to forgive those who have wronged you no matter how serious the wrong they've done to you, for until you do, you'd be carrying your anger and resentment on your back, making it too difficult for you to make even just one step forward.

And while it's true that to forgive someone isn't as easy and as simple as saying "Yes, you're forgiven," forgiveness is a gift that you can actually give to yourself once you have had the time to heal from your pain and resentment.

Listen to "A Bag of Nails," a story by an anonymous writer about hurting others with one's bad temper.

It goes like this:

"Once upon a time there was a little boy with a bad temper. His father gave him a bag of nails and told him that every time he lost his temper, he should hammer a nail in the fence. The first day the boy had driven 37 nails into the fence. But gradually, the number of daily nails dwindled down. He discovered it was easier to hold his temper than to drive those nails into the fence.

"Finally, the first day came when the boy didn't lose his temper at all. He proudly told his father about it and the father suggested that the boy now pull out one nail for each day that he was able to hold his temper. The days passed and the young boy was finally able to tell his father that all the nails were gone.

"The father took his son by the hand and led him to the fence. 'You have done well, my son, but look at the holes in the fence. The fence will never be the same. When you say things in anger, they leave a scar just like this one. You can put a knife in a man and draw it out, it won't matter how many times you say 'I'm sorry,' the wound is still there."

The moral of the story is that you need to curb your temper to avoid hurting others. If you don't hurt others, then worrying about having to be forgiven won't find any room in your life at all.

CHAPTER 20

To Succeed, You Must Persevere

*"Many of life's failures are people who did not realize how close they were to success when they gave up."—**Thomas Alva Edison, great American inventor and businessman who developed many devices in electric power generation, mass sound recording, and motion pictures (1847-1931)***

Have you ever tried working on something you liked but gave up easily because you thought the task was just too tough to accomplish? If you answered "yes," then you're someone who lacks the spirit of perseverance.

Perseverance is making the effort to walk from your car to find help instead of just hoping for someone to pass by when you've run out of gas in an isolated, snowed-out place and you don't have enough clothing for the extreme cold.

Hardly anyone in this world gets handouts for life. For most of us, it's a constant day-to-day struggle for survival in which we fail and sometimes succeed. But do you push through when you're struggling or easily lose hope and give up the moment you hit a snag? That's the big difference between having persistence or perseverance when you're pursuing something you want or need.

Persistence is just doing a difficult task but always with a time limit for reaching a goal, like the short-lived efforts done by a telemarketer or debt collector. On the other hand, perseverance is making the effort to carry out a difficult task without stopping until it's clearly done to the doer's total satisfaction. When we successfully overcome the storms of the long-term journey called life, it's not because of our persistence but our perseverance.

Persistence doesn't necessarily yield positive results; in fact, that yield could even be negative or distasteful. Take my own case to illustrate this very important point.

When I was just a toddler in the 1960s, I was a very fastidious and over-demanding kid. Every time I was brought inside the toy section of a department store, I'd endlessly badger my Dad to buy me every expensive toy that caught my fancy. I'd bawl over and cry out at the top of my lungs until my father gave in to my demands.

That behavior of mine definitely wasn't a good or desirable kind of persistence. Yes, I almost always succeeded in my goal of bringing home those frivolous toys, but you can imagine how devastating its effect was on my exasperated Dad!

Looking back, I realize with great embarrassment what a waste of money it was to buy me those toys that I'd just smash and throw away once I got bored playing with them!

True and useful perseverance is when you continue to pursue or engage in a business that you love but don't have enough technical knowhow and financial muscle to make it prosper. Even when it looks impossible and hopeless, you deal with the tough challenges with grit and fortitude because you love what you're doing and envision yourself becoming a successful entrepreneur if you just tried hard enough.

The best analogy I could think of to illustrate the difference between persistence and perseverance is when you're faced with the problem of wanting to open a padlocked door.

When you can't find the key to get inside the room and you look for a hammer outright and forcibly break the door, that's persistence. But when you're patient enough to look for that key even if it takes a longer time to find it, that's perseverance.

I must confess that when my Dad died of complications from asthma in October 1973 when I was just in high school, I was so emotionally devastated that I lost my desire to continue my studies. For a long time I just confined myself inside the house, never even going out for so many days, telling my Mom again and again that I'm not going to school anymore and that no force in the world could force me to do otherwise.

But in time I awakened to the reality that even with my Dad gone, my life had to go on the way he wanted it to be. I knew that if my Dad were alive, he'd hate it so much if I gave up. He wanted me to be strong, to keep on going, to chase my dreams, and to become the person that I wanted to be even in his absence.

It was with these thoughts in mind that with my Dad's passing, I decided to change the negative attitude that had grown in me. Regaining my positive outlook, I resumed my high school studies and finished it. I persevered in my schooling and obtained my B.S. Commerce degree, took a masteral degree in Business Management, and subsequently also a doctoral degree in Human Resources Management.

You can achieve your dreams and goals in life if you persevere and conquer your fear of failure. Indeed, perseverance is the key; it is the power that can drive you to push forward despite overwhelming difficulties.

Think of J. K. Rowling, the British author of the series of seven *Harry Potter* novels, published between 1997 and 2007, that eventually made her a multimillionaire. Her fortune in 2020 was estimated at £795 million (over US$1 billion), ranking her as the 178th richest person in the United Kingdom.

According to J.K. Rowling herself, "By every usual standard, I was the biggest failure I knew." For seven years in the 1990s she was jobless and living on benefits, suffering from depression after a failed marriage, and taking care of a baby daughter that she had no means to feed.

Her first Harry Potter book had been rejected 12 times by her prospective publishers. As fate would have it, however, the editor of Bloomsbury Publishing just happened to bring home Rowling's manuscript of *Harry Potter and the Philosopher's Stone* that he was reviewing for publication. He was lukewarm about the prospects of that book, but her 8-year-old daughter came across its manuscript and was so fascinated by it that she convinced her father to publish the novel.

So, despite her having been advised that she wouldn't make any money writing children's books, Rowling proved everyone wrong by becoming the first female author in history to become a billionaire.

Let me close this chapter by sharing with you this very instructive and inspiring story written by an anonymous author on the power of perseverance:

"One day a farmer's donkey fell down into a well. The animal cried for hours as the farmer tried to figure out what to do. Finally, he decided the animal was old, and the well needed to be covered up anyway; it just wasn't worth it to retrieve the donkey.

"He invited all his neighbors to come over and help him. They all grabbed a shovel and began to shovel dirt into the well. At first, the donkey realized what was happening and cried even more. Then, to everyone's amazement he quieted down.

"A few shovels load later, the farmer finally looked down the well. He was astonished at what he saw. With each shovel of dirt that hit his back, the donkey was doing something amazing. He would shake it off and take a step up.

"As the farmer's neighbors continued to shovel dirt on top of the animal, he would shake it off and take another step up. Pretty soon, everyone was amazed as the donkey stepped up over the edge of the well and happily trotted off!"

The moral of that story?

It is that life is like a well into which you've fallen. Well-intentioned people are going to shovel all kinds of dirt onto that well to save you, but the best you can do is to take out the dirt by shaking it off from you every time, then make a step up on the growing mound of dirt when it gets high enough so you can get out of the well.

CHAPTER 21

You Must Believe In Yourself

"To be yourself in a world that is constantly trying to make you something else is the greatest accomplishment."
—Oprah Gail Winfrey, American talk show host, television producer, actress, author, and philanthropist
(Born 1954)

Your immediate superior has given you an important and unique project because he believes in your capability. Overwhelmed by its magnitude, you get scared to accept the task instead of taking it as recognition of your preceding good work performance.

You are frightened that you'd prove incapable of producing good quality work. Even worse, your mind has started to swirl with negative thoughts about how your boss and coworkers would jeer and secretly laugh at you once you've failed.

Is this grim career situation reflective of how you view yourself?

One of the reasons why we cower in times of opportunity and big challenge is our self-doubt. It makes us feel incapable of doing things we deem necessary to fulfill our goal. Sadly, society has conditioned us to allow too much self-doubt to occupy a big part of our lives.

There are many factors that could erode our self-confidence even as we are growing up. During our childhood, our parents every now and then would tell us not to continue with what we want to do because we're just not good enough. We allow the opinion of others to drown our own inner voice, and so when doing a task, we have a bad habit of needlessly comparing ourselves to other people.

When you want to do something bigger in your life, do you have the courage to believe in yourself? After all the negativity and pummeling you got as you grew to adulthood, do you still retain the much-needed self-confidence to overcome the many obstacles that life will throw at you?

I've always asked myself those questions when about to do something out of the ordinary. Whether confident or not, I'd always tell myself, "Yes I do!", "But of course I do!" Yet when the moment I'd acted on that resolve but started to encounter road bumps along the way, I'd stop, my self-confidence devastated to a point that I'd feel being squeezed smaller and smaller inside a tiny cage!

Later I'd try to rebuild my self-confidence by educating myself on how some remarkably successful people have managed to survive life's challenges and thrived. I would read countless self-help books, watch social media from early evening till next morning, attend a string of seminars, and even join associations of likeminded people seeking deliverance from their doubts and fears of ever accomplishing anything worthwhile.

From that vantage point, I discovered that many successful individuals have one thing in common—they had failed so miserably before they achieved success. They first learned that they must have the courage to learn to believe in themselves, then made sure they clearly understood that their every failure, rather than a hindrance, could serve as their best tutors in life.

After failing a few of times myself in some small, ill-starred business ventures, I started asking myself this nagging question: "Why are some people successful and others are not?"

My mind sometimes would nudge me with this shouted but silent admonition: "Perhaps you just did something wrong along the way!"

Back then, however, it was difficult to respond to that probing, spur-of-the-moment response. You just couldn't do it when you're angry and upset and your mind is clouded with uncertainty.

Today, when I ask myself that same question and my mind is clear and uncluttered with bitterness over my plans and ventures that didn't work, I'd say to myself unhesitatingly: "Well, unlike those who succeeded in the same situation, I hadn't given myself a chance to discover my true potential and to fearlessly pursue my passion with great dedication and hard work."

During my college days in Cebu City in the late 1970s, we had a classmate whom we could frankly say was at the bottom of our class—he was our "class goat," so to speak. That guy was a notorious troublemaker to us his fellow students, to the teachers, and to the school authorities. Because he did so many bad and unsavory things in school, all of us had adjudged him as a hopeless person who absolutely would have no future.

How wrong we all were in our estimation of him! Today, he's a very successful entrepreneur and is undoubtedly one of the wealthiest graduates of our alma mater. So what brought about this amazing transformation?

In one of our recent college reunions, the now dapper and very respectable-looking guy shared us a very insightful story. When we were undergraduates, he admitted, he knew that he was weak academically and developed a severe inferiority complex as a result. To cover up for these inadequacies, he projected the macho image of a campus troublemaker as a defense mechanism.

Sure, he said, he encountered lots of failure and rejections in life owing to his personal weaknesses but he refused to let failure defeat him. He learned to believe in himself and just kept moving on, never letting his failures prevent him from succeeding and fulfilling his vision in life.

Indeed, in our pursuit of discovering our true inner potential, the best preparation is to develop our character and personal values and to take advantage of the lessons from our mistakes. We have to continue acquiring skills that can be learned from real-life experiences outside the four corners of the classroom.

You have to be very wary if you don't have self-confidence and are a chronic self-doubter. When you suffer from both these handicaps, you won't feel good about yourself every day and you'll be prone to depression. The strongest and most effective antibodies for defeating this twin-headed virus is simple—make every effort to overcome your self-doubt and develop your self-confidence to the fullest.

To bring this chapter to a close, I'm now sharing with you the following 13 thirteen steps for overcoming self-doubt and for building self-confidence:

THE 13 KEYS FOR OVERCOMING SELF-DOUBT AND BUILDING SELF-CONFIDENCE

1. **Always express gratitude.** Appreciate all the things that happen to you. They might be good things or bad things. Small or big, just remember appreciating your capabilities and learning lessons from these things. They will give you a bigger room for improvement.

2. **Stop regretting.** When you keep on blaming yourself for the wrong choices you've made, you'll tend to procrastinate because you'll fear that the same bad things might happen again to you. When you move forward, you'll begin to trust yourself and decide what's right for you.

3. **Tell yourself "I CAN" instead of "I CAN'T."** Establish a self-belief system that anything that comes in your life is given to you by the Almighty because you can handle it.

4. **Try to be a chronic optimist.** By always being positive, you won't be afraid in your life's journey because you'll always see the glass always full of water and not empty.

5. **Establish self-awareness.** When you're always aware of yourself, you know what you're capable of and know your limitations as well. Self-awareness can enrich your emotional intelligence as well as your listening and other communications skills.

6. **Reset your mindset.** When you reset the bad memories of your past, you'll see every new circumstance as if it's your first time, and you won't respond to the same old pattern of habits.

7. **Celebrate life.** When you reward yourself for even a small success, you'll feel happy and will try to replicate the same success story in your next journey.

8. **Record your thoughts.** By writing your thoughts in a diary or journal, you'll become aware of what you really want. You'll be able to identify positive and negative self-talk and therefore you

can control your emotions and your fears over your personal inadequacies.

9. **Practice meditation.** When I had a panic attack that I might have contracted the deadly Covid-19 virus because I had a terrible sore throat and a shortness of breath (a false alarm as it turned out), I did a basic breathing technique and simple meditation to help ease my anxiety. Simple daily meditation promotes emotional health and can make you feel calm and refreshed.

10. **Associate yourself with the right people.** When you have low self-esteem, find the right people who can understand your situation and are willing to help you. The right companions will be your support system.

11. **Be kind to yourself and others.** When you love yourself and do a volunteering job, you'll feel happy and satisfied donating your time and efforts for the benefit of others. This way you'll feel good with yourself and develop stronger self-confidence.

12. **Act on your goal without delay.** While you're still motivated, you need to perform your actions for your goal right away; otherwise, the voice of negativity just might start to rock your brain out.

13. **Practice daily incantation.** Incantation is more effective than just affirmation because the words you utter will send a positive signal to every cell of your body and allow your brain to believe what you're saying.

You can best perform incantation in the morning while doing exercise or facing a mirror. You can say "I am amazing!", "I am very confident!", or "I am powerful!" Be sure to believe and mean what you're saying.

The moment you get used to these incantations, they can help you get calm before giving a presentation or speech or going through a job interview that you feel a little nervous about.

Indeed, when you believe in yourself, your inner limitless potential won't be something you need to reach; it will be something just waiting for you to discover.

CHAPTER 22

Encourage and Inspire Others

"I am thankful for all of those who said NO to me. It's because of them I'm doing it myself."—**Albert Einstein, German-born theoretical physicist who developed the Theory of Relativity; winner of the 1921 Nobel Prize in Physics for his discovery of the law of the photoelectric effect (1875-1955)**

How would you feel if someone of known repute and authority in your line of work told you this? "Congratulations for a job well done! I knew you can do it because you have the capability!"

You'd feel elated for sure because these are words of affirmation and encouragement from a knowledgeable person affirming your competence to do a task well. Whether you know that person or not, your spirit is uplifted because the words assure you that other people noticed your ability and that your effort truly matters to them.

The word "encouragement" comes from the combination of the Latin prefix *"en-"* that means "to put into" and the Latin root *"cor"*that means "the heart." This is why the phrase "encouragement goes straight to the heart" is very popular and often used in self-development seminars and training programs.

Getting sincere and merited encouragement from other people gives the receiver pride and joy, automatically making him or her think of reciprocating them for the inspiration they have given.

Psychologists say that when you're motivated by other people's encouragement, you should also fire up your spirit to encourage others. It's a give-and-take situation. Always remember that a well-deserved encouragement, given freely and enthusiastically, causes other people's heart to sing with delight and happiness.

We should make a clear distinction though between proper

encouragement and off hand flattery. Flattery isn't a heartfelt form of praise because it usually comes with wanting something in return from the flattered person. This is why it's very important to give honest and specific encouragement because it's in the nature of people to always know the difference between simple flattery and a compliment that comes from the heart.

In the case of Albert Einstein, the great physicist whose intellectual achievements and originality have made his name synonymous with "genius," he looked at the act of encouragement in a different light.

In a truly magnanimous gesture, he gave recognition to those who refused to recognize his achievements in science or even spurned them. Indeed, he acknowledged without bitterness that their negativity towards his work provided him with the energy, motivation, and inspiration to strive harder in his scientific pursuits.

Michael Jordan, the American professional basketball player and principal owner of the NBA's Charlotte Hornets, demonstrated more or less the same outlook as Albert Einstein's toward his achievements in life.

Listen to Michael's reply when he was asked for the secret to his success: "I'm not competing with other players, but I'm competing with myself, with what I am capable of."

At this point, I'd like to share a personal story of mine about the impact of encouragement to what I've become in my own life.

In the late 1970s, after only a semester of college study in a Cebu City university, I felt a great desire to experience a new life away from home and to study in a more prestigious academic institution.

For this reason, I flew to Manila to see an older niece of mine—I call her Nang Alice—at her Makati City residence. Nang Alice, a very successful entrepreneur who owned The Wonderlands Philippine Hotel in Pasay City, knew why I wanted to see her.

It was because right after my Dad's death in 1973, Nang Alice had offered to help me and my sister Linda when she attended my Dad's wake and internment in Cebu City. There, Nang Alice offered to foot my college studies and even gave me the liberty of choosing which university, and on top of that she offered me a job at her Wonderlands Hotel.

Her offer was an opportunity of a lifetime for me!

As fate would have it, however, my dream was dashed to pieces when I was about to take the entrance exam to the university of my choice. I got a severe ear infection and was stricken with high fever. I later got homesick at Nang Alice's place in Makati and then decided to go back to Cebu to study just one more semester there before going back to Manila. I did this thinking that the opportunity Nang Alice had promised me was still open.

However, when I called her from an uncle's residence in Makati to follow up on her promise, she was too busy and I just couldn't talk to her. She became unreachable for so many days. Her evident refusal to talk to me confused me no end.

The rancor in my heart grew to the point of asking myself this question: "Why is she now reneging on her promise to me?" Back then I didn't see any wisdom in her leaving me on a lurch like that. I felt the pain of rejection and began to doubt her sincerity to help me. I got desperate.

All of a sudden my dream of studying and working in the big city had disappeared like smoke in thin air!

What happened triggered such a powerful desire in me to get out of my comfort zone and to make this firm resolve: Do things on my own and pursue my passion with enthusiasm without expecting help from others.

Motivating myself to find the best part of me, I worked very hard and finished my college degree, earned a master's degree, then even earned a doctorate degree as well.

The bitter lesson I learned from that experience? When opportunity knocks at your door, open that door right away for there might just be no second time around!

Looking back, I can say now without rancor I am thankful for my Nang Alice's rejection of me at that crucial moment in my life. It encouraged me to push myself to my limits. It made me a stronger person capable of weathering the storms of my life all by myself.

What Nang Alice had imparted in me—whether she did it consciously or unconsciously—was this very wise and powerful lesson: I had to develop my character primarily on my own and to become truly independent-minded in my efforts to discover my own true potential.

At this point, let me now share with you 22 ways for encouraging and inspiring people around you to become their best version of themselves.

22 WAYS FOR INSPIRING PEOPLE AROUND YOU TO BECOME THEIR BEST VERSION OF THEMSELVES

1. **Be friendly.** It doesn't necessarily mean that you have to talk to others in order to be friendly. A small gesture like smiling can make their day. Friendly people are never alone because people who need help are abundant.

2. **Expect others to grow.** When you believe on the capabilities of others to discover their potential and shine, you're giving them hope to pursue their goals.

3. **Give credit to others.** When you recognize even the smallest deeds of others, you're uplifting their spirit to continue their journey. This is an excellent form of leadership in the workplace.

4. **Avoid praising yourself.** People won't believe you if you trumpet your own accomplishments, which is bragging that you're superior. Your humility—not your superiority—could encourage others to pursue their own passion.

5. **Be proud of the good work of others.** Becoming proud of someone else's work is motivating them to improve their self-worth and self-confidence—and then motivating them to add more color on their work.

6. **Avoid making false promises.** When you break your promise, people feel unvalued and won't trust you anymore owing to your insincerity. You'll lose your integrity if you keep on deceiving other people.

7. **Show you are vulnerable.** Others will admire you if you are truthful about your shortcomings because they know we're all

human. You'll never be able to inspire people if they see you as too good to be true.

8. **Share your knowledge.** When you share your ideas to people, you empower them to be creative and innovative. They will then acquire the self-confidence that they, too, can pull the trigger.

9. **Listen closely to others.** People will be inspired if you show them that you value their thoughts and feelings.

10. **Tell inspiring stories.** When people hear encouraging stories from you, they'll most likely find creative ways to achieve their goal. This is because the stories you share are a good source for gaining experience and learning the ropes of life.

11. **Offer help to others.** People are motivated to continue their journey if they feel that somebody is willing to give them a helping hand. Practice "carefrontation"—the careful and caring confrontation with others.

12. **Praise people.** If others will hear your affirmation for them, they'd feel good about themselves and would most likely continue doing what they do.

13. **Return the favor.** If somebody did a good deed for you, they'd reciprocate. Every positive action produces positive results.

14. **Lead by example.** If you walk your talk and take calculated risks, people will appreciate you. Practice what you preach or don't preach at all.

15. **Show interest to others.** You build confidence and self-worth if you show interest to what others are doing or talking about.

16. **Be compassionate to others.** You can help others to move forward if you are truly concerned about their welfare. Being compassionate to others will also enable you to understand more about yourself because your perspective will be broadened.

17. **Be optimistic.** When you are happy with who you are, others will let your positivity inspire them. The more positive you feel, the more you can establish better relationships.

18. **Be transparent.** People will always believe in you if you're not hiding something from them. The computer term WYSIWYG

("What You See Is What You Get") is the best definition of transparency.

19. **Let others feel your availability for them.** Feeling that somebody is just beside you anytime you need help can inspire and promote positive behaviors.

20. **Be appreciative of others.** People will feel joy and happy when you make people feel good about themselves. A simple "You're wearing a beautiful pants today" is enough to ignite encouragement.

21. **Always show your composure.** Keeping your cool in difficult and trying situations means you have a strong EQ (emotional quotient), which is a characteristic of successful people.

22. **Give others a pat on the back.** Touch is an effective emotional trigger. When you appreciate somebody by patting their backs, people will be motivated. In the workplace, a pat in the back is equivalent to saying "You did a good job!" It makes people's hearts leap with joy.

Always remember to practice these 22 ways for inspiring the people around you. Giving inspiration to others can make others feel good about themselves and you yourself. Life is so full of struggles so we need to handle the people we deal with tact, courtesy, and understanding.

Encouraging another person is very gratifying but wouldn't it be much better if both of you encourage and inspire each other at the same time? This is what's called "reciprocal encouragement." The giver in turn becomes the receiver, and vice versa.

Here's one more beautiful story about encouragement that I couldn't resist sharing before ending this chapter:

In the 2016 Olympics in Rio de Janeiro, Brazil, two athletes in the 5,000-meter race caught the world's attention. About 3,200 meters into the race, New Zealander Nikki Hamblin and American Abbey D'Agostino collided and fell. Abbey was quickly up on her feet but stopped to help Nikki.

Moments after that, the two athletes started running again, Abbey began faltering though, for her right leg turned out to have been injured owing to the fall. It was now Nikki's turn to stop and help Abbey, steadying and encouraging her to finish the race.

When Abbey eventually stumbled across the finish line, Nikki was waiting to joyfully embrace her.

What a beautiful picture of mutual encouragement that was! Proof positive that everything you need to encourage others already resides in you!

CHAPTER 23

Practice Expressing Your Gratitude

*"Feeling gratitude and not expressing it is like wrapping a present and not giving it."—**William Arthur Ward, prolific American author of inspirational maxims, editor, Christian pastor and teacher (1921-1994)***

Can you recall that time when you told somebody that you were so grateful for his or her support when you were facing serious problems in life? And do you remember how the situation made both of you feel?

First, the person to whom you expressed your gratitude no doubt was elated and joyful for your appreciation of that support. On your part, you verbalized the gladness in your heart for the support that person extended to you. It was a win-win situation that began and ended with heartfelt expressions of gratitude to each other.

Now contrast that situation to another circumstance one weekend sometime ago when I sadly overlooked the need for expressing gratitude. That day in 2013, I keenly looked forward to compete in a big tennis tournament scheduled at the Hill Country Tennis Academy, in Kerville, Texas. I was very excited by the prospect of my playing against my tennis buddies.

However, when I opened the door to go out for my drive to the tournament grounds some 20 kilometers away, I found that it was raining in torrents outside! My self-talk kicked in violently. I began cursing the weather and literally commanded the rain to stop right then and there because if it didn't, the tournament would have to be rescheduled for the next weekend when I'd already be out of town.

"What bad luck and what the heck?" I cursed, thrusting my fist to the high heavens!

It is regrettably this kind of attitude that creates situations that attract and trigger negative circumstances in your life, always guaranteeing a bad weekend for you. But truth to tell, it's really something you can avoid by reprogramming your brain to see the better side of life in times like that.

Instead of complaining, which of course is a very unpleasant manifestation of ungratefulness; try to take each day as a blessed day because the fact is that it's not just another day but God's gift of life for you. You're lucky that you still wake up in the morning to once again see the beauty of life.

Yes, the only appropriate response to events that happen in our life is by being grateful, for when we're grateful, we can't be negative and angry.

My immediate boss, the company vice president of the Saudi Aramco affiliate in the city of Al-Khobar where I worked in the early 2000s, used to regale me with this story about the first king of Saudi Arabia:

"Whenever there was rain, the King and the Royal Family would go out to the desert and enjoy dancing in the rain, singing and chanting to give thanks to Allah for the gift of clean water that came direct from heaven."

Truly, there's no right time and place to express our gratitude; we can always use our sense of gratitude anytime and show it anywhere we are.

Many scientific studies have conclusively shown that expressing gratitude produces positive effects to our mind, our emotions, and our body in general. The U.S. publication *The Journal of Positive Psychology* summarizes these scientific findings on the effects of gratitude, as follows:

—Dr. Rollin McCraty and his colleagues conducted a study in 1998 about how to "cultivate appreciation and other positive emotions." Their findings suggest that people with an "attitude of gratitude" experience lower levels of stress.

—In a study by Seligman, Steen, and Peterson (2005), participants were given one week to write and then deliver a letter of thanks in person to someone who had been especially kind to them, but who had never been properly thanked.

The results showed that participants who engaged in the letter-writing exercise reported more happiness for one month after the intervention compared to a control group.

—According to a *Harvard Health Publications* article that summarized the findings of several studies on gratitude, "Managers who remember to say 'thank you' to people who work for them find that those employees feel motivated to work harder."

Based on the above studies, you don't have to incur any personal expense when you invest in creating an attitude of gratitude. All you have to do is your "one-cent act of happiness" and an overflow of gratitude will follow.

By using gratitude as a measure of the creation of a healthy relationship with ourselves, we can likewise similarly establish a healthy relationship with others. When we plant the seeds of thankfulness inside our hearts, we'll surely harvest a bounty of good people living in harmony with one another.

Now, to end this chapter, I'm sharing for your continuing reference 15 simple, tried-and-tested ways to express your attitude of gratitude:

15 SIMPLE, TRIED-AND-TESTED WAYS TO EXPRESS YOUR ATTITUDE OF GRATITUDE

1. **Give a surprise visit.** When you surprise people—family members, friends, or colleagues—with a visit, they'll be grateful that somebody gives them importance.
2. **Always say "Thank you!"** This is one of the easiest ways of expressing gratitude. Thanking someone can create positive emotions and enhance the relationship.
3. **Appreciate what you have in life.** By appreciating who you are and what you have, you'll improve your perspective in life. Even if you don't have money but you are healthy, it's reason enough for you to be thankful of what you have. When you appreciate everything you now have, you'll stop complaining about what's lacking in your life.

4. **Offer help to others.** When you're willing to help others, it will give you a sense of renewal and inner peace because you'll make someone happy. I want to emphasize that helping others doesn't necessarily require you to share your financial abundance. Even if you're poor, you can extend your help through your creative ideas and through sharing your time and efforts with others.

5. **Give small surprise gifts.** When you give somebody an unexpected gift, no matter how small it is, your gesture will make him or her happy. Giving someone a concert ticket is a unique gift, too.

6. **Be kind to others.** Showing your kindness to others, even to animals, will have doubly beneficial effects to you and to them. That's the feeling of satisfaction.

7. **Smile to strangers.** When you give your smiles to strangers, you'll make them comfortable because you show an essence of "approachability." On your part, you'll trigger a happy mood in your brain.

8. **Respect others.** Respecting others doesn't necessarily mean that you like everything in a person. Showing respect for who they are regardless of their inadequacies or failings will create an atmosphere of fairness and trust. In the workplace, respect can motivate staff to work harder and become more productive.

9. **Join community service.** Volunteering your time and effort will connect you to others, and this can make your world and theirs a better place. Scientific research has found that volunteerism increases levels of happiness, self-esteem, and life-satisfaction.

10. **Practice a positive attitude.** Being an optimistic person could make you more resilient in facing difficulties. Positive people have more friends and influence; thus, by being positive yourself, more people will support you in your undertakings. Having a positive attitude can make you accomplish more than what negative-thinking people can.

11. **Communicate with others.** You can send e-mail or a text message, or maybe chat with friends or colleagues who haven't contacted you for some time; they will be grateful to you for

your gesture. Communication is engagement and when you engage, you improve relationships. In the workplace, good communication improves team-building and clarifies goals.

12. **Be a good listener.** People will be happy when they feel that someone is interested about their feelings and thoughts. Remember that listening is the beginning of understanding and respect.

13. **Invite others over a cup of coffee.** Going out of your way to invite a friend or colleague to talk over a cup of coffee could enhance your personal connection and improve your relationship.

14. **Encourage others.** Inspiring others could change their outlook in life; it gives them hope to accomplish what they are doing.

15. **Practice gratitude challenge.** Doing gratitude challenge is a healthy form of activities beneficial to everyone. A relative of mine accepted a 20-day challenge to do 40 push-ups daily for 30 days and posted it on Facebook to show proof. He successfully finished the 30 days.

When I asked him about the experience, he told me that he enjoyed the routine and was thankful that the 20-day challenge made these three wonderful things possible for him: (a) he established a sense of time management; (b) he learned to fulfill a promise; and (c) he developeda chest muscle for which he was grateful.

Truly, expressing gratitude not only helps you appreciate what you've received but also makes you honestly feel that you're giving something back to others for their kindness.

CHAPTER 24

Demonstrate Your Social Responsibility

"We make a living by what we get, but we make a life by what we give."—Sir Winston Churchill, British Prime Minister from 1940 to 1945 (1874-1965)

We are created by the Almighty to exist in harmony with one another, so all of us have an obligation to take care not only of ourselves but also of other people and society in general.

Social responsibility goes hand-in-hand with ethics, of course. Any organization, whether for profit or non-profit, must be ethically principled to survive, thrive, and succeed in the long term.

There are two types of social responsibility: business responsibility, and individual responsibility.

Business social responsibility, which as we know is more commonly known as corporate social responsibility, is the obligation of businessmen to society. Peter F. Drucker, the Austrian-born American management consultant, educator, and author who is acknowledged as the founder of modern management, defined this obligation of business as follows:

"Social responsibility requires managers to consider whether their action is likely to promote the public good, to advance the basic beliefs of our society, to contribute to its stability, strength and harmony."

There is no formal specific term for an individual's responsibility, but I would call it "our personal social responsibility to our community."

As a whole, I believe that social responsibility is the duty of individuals and companies to act in the best interests of society as a whole and of their environment as well.

But how is social responsibility not exercised or selflessly exercised or in our daily lives?

In our place in Lapu-Lapu City there's a woman—let's just call her Maria Conchita (not her real name) to protect her identity—who built a row of residential apartments in her block. When she started to build the apartment, other residents in homes close to it appealed to her to give them at least a small pathway to pass through going to the *main road*.

But their appeals fell into deaf ears. Maria Conchita sternly refused and told them these words: "I can do anything I want because it's my property."

Maria Conchita proceeded to have her apartment built. It occupied every inch of her lot until its perimeter, giving the other residents no option other than to encroach on other people's property or to take the very far road going to the highway.

Fortunately for them, the owner of the property adjacent to Maria Conchita's allowed them to pass through his property; he even promised them that he would keep the passageway permanently open for them even when he becomes financially capable of building a house or apartment on his property.

That other property owner's personal principle was this: "We should share every small thing that we have with our poor brethren, for after all, we couldn't bring the property with us when we finally go six feet below the ground."

This, I would say, is a clear example of "personal social irresponsibility."

The need to be socially responsible often comes in the form of guilt that you feel when you're not able to personally help distraught fellow Filipinos when you see them on TV news struck by calamitous typhoons or floods in Metro Manila or elsewhere in the country. I'm not sure exactly how you feel watching such situations, but I do feel guilty that I'm just watching and I couldn't be there to help and alleviate their suffering.

Even if I decide to donate personal funds through some humanitarian organization, I find it emotionally satisfying to be there personally giving hands-on help. For me, one's presence is infinitely better than just giving a material donation. Sometimes, tears would just fall from my eyes because I'm unable to actually help. This could be owing to the fact that when I was in elementary school and high school I was very enthusiastic to become a priest, but everything changed when my Dad died in 1973 when I was only in second year high.

On September 26, 2009, when tropical storm Ondoy devastated Metro Manila with extreme flooding that drowned 288 people, I happened to be in Balanga, Bataan, as the dean of business administration of the Asia Pacific College of Advanced Studies. I thought of going alone to Metro Manila to see how I could help, but then the owner and president of our college, Mrs. Flocerfida E. Ayangco.

Madam Flocerfida declared a one-day school holiday so its faculty and staff could extend help to the typhoon victims.

Mrs. Flocerfida arranged for all of the college deans and faculty members to be transported to the GMA TV warehouse in Quezon City, 114.3 kilometers away. There, all of us helped pack hundreds of kilos of rice and corn, then brought the food packs ourselves to the flood-hit areas.

After a whole day of packing rice and corn into food bags and manually distributing to so many of the flood-hit recipients, I thought I'd get so physically exhausted when I got back to my apartment in Balanga, Bataan. I expected to just collapse in bed due to sheer exhaustion.

But the truth was that I didn't feel any iota of exhaustion at all when I got back to my apartment! After dinner, in fact, I even treated myself to a bottle of beer in a nearby restaurant. Instead of getting exhausted to the bone, I remained alert and very happy and gratified for what I did during that day! It was probably because for such a long time, my mind before that day was like being inside a prison cell not caring for anybody's interest and welfare except my own.

I now also remember that in 2013 when I was working in Middle East, I had a circle of Filipino friends in the Kingdom of Bahrain who would help run away Filipina domestic helpers get back to the Philippines. It was the norm for Middle East employers to keep the passports of domestic helpers the moment they'd start working, so when their employer happens to maltreat them they might be able to flee from but absolutely couldn't travel out of the country back to their homeland.

Our closely-knit Filipino circle had a friend at the time—let's just call him Johnny—who had established a close friendship with an influential Bahraini national that we'll just name Abdulrahman here to protect his identity.

Abdulrahman worked in one of the government offices in Bahrain, and whenever a runaway Filipina domestic helper was seeking help from other than the Philippine Embassy, Johnny would inform his Bahraini friend about her plight.

The modus operandi of Abdulrahman was this: He would inform the employer that his runaway Filipina domestic helper was currently in jail. Most employers would be happy being told that because they usually would come out with sleazy stories against their Filipina helper, often that she had ran away not from his maltreatment and abuse but because she was stealing cash or jewelries from him and his family.

At this point, Abdulrahman would ask the employer if he would be willing to pay the three-times-a-day meal expenses for the Filipina domestic helper, for it was the rule in Bahrain that the employer should shoulder all the meal expenses for the person they wanted to be incarcerated.

Almost none of the employers would want to spend a Bahraini dinar for that purpose, of course, so they'd refuse to pay for the domestic helper's meal allowance. When this happens, Abdulrahman would politely ask the employer to return the domestic helper's passport and the employers would invariably return it.

This done, the Philippine Embassy would process and the passport within more or less a week and the runaway Filipina would soon be able to fly back to the Philippines. (In contrast, if the runaway Filipina domestic helper would go directly to the Philippine Embassy, it would take her about four to six months before she could go home. Sometimes some unscrupulous Filipino staff inside the embassy would even take advantage of her.)

Once the Philippine embassy had already processed the Filipina domestic helper's passport, it was the turn of our circle of Filipino friends to chip in for her plane fare to the Philippines. A fellow Filipino contact working as an airline agent would make a tentative flight booking. We would also buy some chocolates for our unfortunate *kababayan* so she would at least have some *pasalubong* for her family back in the homeland.

Usually, too, female friends of the Filipina domestic helper would hand to her all of our donated goodies and all of her personal belongings once the Bahraini police had set her free at the airport. This was because she was forbidden to go back to her employer's place to get her things.

Still on the subject of social responsibility, sometime in 1998 when our Middle East head office assigned me to the Saudi Aramco Jeddah Refinery, my fellow Filipinos based in Jeddah organized a group whose name I myself coined: the Cebuano Speaking Organization in Saudi Arabia, or CSOSA.(The name sounds Cebuano but some members were married a person from different parts of the Philippines, so COSA was actually a mixed regional grouping.)

The main goal of CSOSA was to gather as many Filipinos as possible in devising and implementing a plan to effectively help beleaguered fellow Pinoys in that faraway Arab land. For this purpose, we called a general assembly from around 40 places near and far from Jeddah, which was the biggest city in Saudi Arabia and with the biggest land area.

Because it was a Friday and a worker's day off, the CSOSA general assembly was attended by almost a hundred Filipinos. It wasn't easy to call a meeting again of that magnitude, so all of the attendees unanimously agreed to elect the Board Members and President right then and there.

The CSOSA elected me as its president, with one of my major advocacies that of helping our fellow Filipino OFWs who'd be going home to the Philippines but would have huge financial problems in doing so.

During one of our meetings to make the organization's by-laws, that idea of mine was disapproved because some of the elected officers opposed the idea of spending their money for our own distressed OFW CSOSA members in Saudi Arabia. In the end, however, my proposal was ratified when I explained that no specific amount of contribution would be set; contributions of any amount would be voluntary and the organization's fund won't be used for the purpose.

As fate would have it, little did I know that I myself would become the first beneficiary of that particular CSOSA by-law that just happened to be my personal advocacy.

Back in the Philippines after I left Jeddah in the year 2000, my youngest son was admitted to the hospital for a physical impairment at a time that I had no gainful work. How surprised I was that the CSOSA president who took over from me wrote me e-mail that was truly Heaven-sent! He said that a fellow CSOSA member was going home and that I had to come to their house in Quezon City to accept some financial assistance pitched in by CSOSA members in Jeddah. That financial assistance meant a lot to me because it helped defray the cost of my son's hospitalization.

"You reap what you sow."

I have always believed in that ancient proverb. Yes, it tells us that in life, you'll always get what you deserve; whatever you've put your time, skill, and energy into is what you'll get back.

To end this chapter, I now would like to quote from Carrie Marie Underwood, the American country music singer, songwriter, record producer, and actress who rose to prominence after winning the fourth season of the TV show *American Idol* in 2005.

Carrie said: "Successful people have a social responsibility to make the world a better place and not just take from it."

EPILOGUE

The objective of this book, *Pathways to Achieving Your Fullest Potential*, is to provide you with a wealth of insights for reinventing yourself to become the best possible person you can be.

Everything in your life is controlled by the power of your own mindset. Like your laptop or desktop, you need to periodically reprogram and upgrade your brain's software so you can see in full clarity all of the things that you've been before and those you're now capable of doing today. If you use the power of your creative imagination, anything you want to accomplish would be possible.

In fact, it has been scientifically shown that people who simply imagined—yes, simply imagined!—practicing the piano every day physically strengthened the muscles in their fingers. That is how powerful our brain can be as to make it possible for us to reinvent ourselves.

But no matter how much more perceptive, productive, and progressive you'll become after reading this book, never forget to pause every so often to enjoy and celebrate life whether you're alone, with your loved ones, with your associates at work, or with your trusted companions and friends.

You owe it to yourself to celebrate your unique, one-way journey in this life. Don't be too hard to yourself and don't take life too seriously either; embrace every new day by rewarding yourself and sharing your bounties with those who badly need and deserve them.

The best way to make your life worth living is to build a life of your choice, but always be sure that what you're doing and enjoying as result of your efforts are likewise helping in some measure to promote the well-being and comfort of the other people in this world.

Good luck and best wishes for success in your life and in your career or calling!

Printed in the United States
by Bookmasters

Printed in the United States
By Bookmasters